ADVANCE PR...

ATYPICAL

"Brilliant, creative writing. His next book should be a novel."
—Temple Grandin, PhD,
author of *Thinking in Pictures*

"With a voice as keen and honest as any I've ever had the pleasure of reading, Jesse Saperstein cracks open the underbelly of life with Asperger's, mesmerizing readers with a tale that is as fabulously incorrigible as it is strikingly compelling. Jesse Saperstein is the son I always wanted!"
—Liane Holliday Willey,
author of *Pretending to Be Normal*

"This funny, poignant, and honest book provides further evidence that Asperger's syndrome is no cookie-cutter diagnosis. *Atypical* also informs us that Jesse Saperstein is a wonderful addition to the world of Asperger literature."
—Michael John Carley,
executive director of the Global and Regional Asperger Syndrome Partnership (GRASP) and author of *Asperger's From the Inside Out*

"Honest, funny, bristling with ideas and intelligence, Jesse A. Saperstein's *Atypical* marks the debut of a bright young voice from the Asperger's community."
—Tim Page,
author of *Parallel Play* and professor
at the University of Southern California

continued

"Amusing, surprising, and informative. Just when I thought I had learned all I can from personal accounts, I had the chance to read this one!"

—Jerry Newport,
author of *Mozart and the Whale*,
with Mary Newport and Johnny Dodd

"Jesse Saperstein's wise and compelling memoir lets us know how frustrating and strange life can be for a bright, resourceful young man with Asperger's navigating the typical world. Funny, irreverent, and ultimately forgiving of all the damage we 'well-adjusted' typicals wreak on those who are a little different from us."

—Sigourney Weaver, actress

"By describing his experience with honesty, passion, and deep clarity, Saperstein allows a so-called neurotypical like myself to completely identify with his atypicality. A very powerful read."

—Bruce Altman, actor

"Jesse Saperstein is witty, insightful, and smart. He is also caring, social, emotional, empathetic, and able to learn from his mistakes and other people's rudeness—all traits we are often told that people with Asperger's don't have. I highly recommend this book to parents, educators, community members—frankly, to everyone. Jesse, I want to know what happens next; I hope you are working on a sequel!"

—Chantal Sicile-Kira,
author of *Autism Spectrum Disorders* and *Autism Life Skills*

ATYPICAL

LIFE WITH ASPERGER'S
IN 20⅓ CHAPTERS

JESSE A. SAPERSTEIN

A Perigee Book

A PERIGEE BOOK
Published by the Penguin Group
Penguin Group (USA) Inc.
375 Hudson Street, New York, New York 10014, USA

Penguin Group (Canada), 90 Eglinton Avenue East, Suite 700, Toronto, Ontario M4P 2Y3, Canada
(a division of Pearson Penguin Canada Inc.)
Penguin Books Ltd., 80 Strand, London WC2R 0RL, England
Penguin Group Ireland, 25 St. Stephen's Green, Dublin 2, Ireland (a division of Penguin Books Ltd.)
Penguin Group (Australia), 250 Camberwell Road, Camberwell, Victoria 3124, Australia
(a division of Pearson Australia Group Pty. Ltd.)
Penguin Books India Pvt. Ltd., 11 Community Centre, Panchsheel Park, New Delhi—110 017, India
Penguin Group (NZ), 67 Apollo Drive, Rosedale, North Shore 0632, New Zealand
(a division of Pearson New Zealand Ltd.)
Penguin Books (South Africa) (Pty.) Ltd., 24 Sturdee Avenue, Rosebank, Johannesburg 2196,
South Africa
Penguin Books Ltd., Registered Offices: 80 Strand, London WC2R 0RL, England

While the author has made every effort to provide accurate telephone numbers and Internet addresses at
the time of publication, neither the publisher nor the author assumes any responsibility for errors, or for
changes that occur after publication. Further, the publisher does not have any control over and does not
assume any responsibility for author or third-party websites or their content.

First edition: April 2010

Library of Congress Cataloging-in-Publication Data

Saperstein, Jesse A.
    Atypical : life with Asperger's in 20 1/3 chapters / Jesse A. Saperstein.
        p.   cm.
    ISBN 978-0-399-53572-7
    1. Saperstein, Jesse A.—Mental health.   2. Asperger's syndrome—Patients—United States—
Biography.   I. Title.
    RC553.A88S27 2010
    362.196'8588320092—dc22   2009047525
    [B]

PRINTED IN THE UNITED STATES OF AMERICA

10 9 8 7 6 5 4 3 2 1

This book describes the real experiences of real people. The author has disguised the identities of some,
and in some instances created composite characters, but none of these changes has affected the
truthfulness and accuracy of his story. Penguin is committed to publishing works of quality and integrity.
In that spirit, we are proud to offer this book to our readers; however, the story, the experiences, and the
words are the author's alone.

*For Joey DiPaolo and all the campers
of Camp Teens Living a Challenge (TLC).
You were the original catalyst
for everything profound that followed.*

*And for my grandfather
Dr. Robert Ernest Colby,
who helped me conclude this story.*

CONTENTS

Introduction   ix

First Impressions   1

The Cards We Are Dealt   11

Cat-Shit Fantasies and Holiday Greetings   21

Empathy: Real, Artificial, and Different   31

The Inability to Let Go   43

Bar Mitzvah Memories   53

Millerton Days   63

Elizabeth West   73

Collegiate Challenges   85

Psychobabble   95

All the World's an Awkward Stage   105

Teens Living a Greater Challenge   113

Summiting the Stigma   127

A Fractured Fairy Tale   143

Weirdish Romance   155

Listies   167

Speaking Out   173

A Brush with Hollywood   187

A Grave Situation   201

Epilogue   215

Acknowledgments   221

INTRODUCTION

My earliest childhood memory takes place in a hospital room at age two and a half after the birth of my sister, Dena. She was born on Halloween, of all days, which was an ominous precursor to her Scorpio personality. I was running around the hospital room to release some pent-up energy, as my mother lay helpless in her Percodan-stoned condition. With no other adults in the room to stop me, I found the controls under her bed and ecstatically began operating the mechanical beast with my poor mother along for the ride. It was a novel curiosity how a bed could become animated, and I had the power to manipulate its movements. She handed me a purple stuffed animal to disarm my antics—one of those innocuous monsters from *Sesame Street* with a bulbous, plastic nose. It produced a silly noise when squeezed. This diversion took my attention away from the bed as annoying, honking sounds filled the room.

As a toddler, my development was atypical—for someone born with a disability. My mother even had reason to believe I was a genius! At eighteen months, I had already mastered the alphabet, simple arithmetic, and shapes. I was also extremely verbal and affectionate, which (back then) were not typical symptoms of what I would come to be diagnosed with more than ten years later. The most abnormal thing about me was a complete lack of interest in imaginative play, which frustrated my mother, who had spent a small fortune buying me toys. She purchased all the Fisher-Price Little People, with their coifed, plastic manes and hollow chambers where their asses should have been. But I had no interest in them.

When I attended a Vassar College nursery school program at age three, my teachers immediately sensed that something was wrong. I avoided socializing with other children, and making eye contact was as uncomfortable as staring into the blazing sun. Other times, I would pause in the middle of a jigsaw puzzle to vigorously flap my hands. And when I wished to communicate a message to one of the other children, I would do so by pushing them or grabbing their Hess trucks. My mother observed this behavior behind the one-way mirror, but was not ready to entertain the notion of a disability. My teachers recommended she take me to a local neurologist, who dismissed my behavior as a temporary developmental delay. When another child psychologist claimed she saw some "autistic-like tendencies," my mother had to restrain herself from slapping the woman who dared insinuate I had something as devastating as autism. *Children with autism are emotionally distant and unaware of their surround-*

ings. They scream without provocation and engage in self-injurious behavior. But I had none of these characteristics, and my parents felt justified to linger in the bliss of denial.

I was six years old when my parents brought me to a famed neurologist at Columbia University. His caliber was so renowned that people thought of him as a scientific fortune-teller who could determine whether a child's future would be filled with hope or heartache. I vaguely remember the doctor's office and the large, white-haired man who briefly examined me. My maternal grandmother accompanied us so that she could babysit me in the waiting room as my parents met with the doctor after the examination. In the waiting room, she presented me with a drawstring bag. I reached inside and withdrew a handful of magnetic marbles that clamored to bind together in one jumbled mass. I tried turning one of the marbles over to make the nonmagnetic side stick to one of the others. It did not work due to a mysterious force repelling them from one another. Plenty of six-year-olds would have recognized the pointlessness of trying to conquer this invisible power, although I continued to push anyway. Most of my life has entailed "pushing against a force," with perpetually frustrating outcomes.

The vacuous, relentless quest for answers would be placed on a back burner for eight more years after the white-haired doctor diagnosed me with a condition called hyperlexia. The neurologist also referred to it as "*Sesame Street* syndrome," because small children with hyperlexia display unusual skills in areas like letter/number recognition and are often early readers. While this condition superficially seems like a gift as opposed to a disability, most hyperlexic children have poor social skills. I was also diagnosed with static encephalopathy, which is a form of brain damage.

Even though these diagnoses were correct, they did not point to the main issue at hand. But the doctor was right about one thing.

"Academically . . . things should fall into place with Jesse. But his greatest hurdle in life will be his social skills and relationships with others."

Like countless other children, I fell through the cracks. It was my misfortune to have been born in 1982—twelve years before Asperger's syndrome was officially recognized as an American disability. Another reason it took so long for us to receive an accurate diagnosis was that my problems were usually not severe enough to warrant psychological intervention. And when I did have problems, they were always most tenacious during periods of transition. New schools, strange peers, and other compounding changes were enough to conjure up my social demons. My problems tended to subside once I became acclimated to my new surroundings and my peers got used to my quirks. Ninth grade was the freakish exception.

The transition into high school produced an unrelenting tempest of academic and social miseries. Considering that bullying typically peaks by eighth or ninth grade, my peers apparently found it necessary to create one last, prolonged orgasm of teenage malice. The worst of it occurred in the Biology Class from Hell. On a good day, the bullying was tolerable and even humorous. One afternoon, I parted my binder to discover someone had inserted a photo of Aladdin giving Princess Jasmine anal pleasure with huge Disney smiles plastered on their faces. Most of the time, however, lessons on cellular mitosis were combined with sharp kicks to my ass cheeks while I deftly ducked spitballs flung in my direction. These aspiring sociopaths forced our poor fifty-year-old teacher into early retirement. In addition to my social problems, I was barely passing my Regents-level Math and Biology classes.

When my parents forced me back into therapy, it seemed like a punishment heaped upon an already toxic school year. I despised therapists almost as much as school. What good did they do except serving as a vortex of time and money while failing to solve my problems? But this particular therapist was actually a medical school–educated psychiatrist who was able to provide more constructive feedback than the usual "Stop perseverating, Jesse!" He had the progressive insight to diagnose me with Asperger's syndrome, as opposed to merely lecturing me about negative energy.

When the psychiatrist gave us the diagnosis, I thought he said, "Ass Burgers." It sounded like a slang term for a bowel movement or a deposit of anal fungus induced by extremely poor personal hygiene.

"Asperger's syndrome is the mildest form of autism," he explained. "This is why you have so many social problems and speak in a flat, monotone voice."

Before someone made them official with an actual name, my problems seemed too benign and intermittent to be classified as a disability. On the other hand, I was too different to be considered normal. It is a central irony of my life that my greatest disabler has been to live with a disability so profoundly mild that people do not usually identify it as more than a character flaw. Its abnormality screams out to the public without someone to give it a proper voice.

My experience with high-functioning autism has been a roller coaster of extremes. The journey has forced me into quagmires of chronic failure and bitterness that have lasted up to years at a time. On the other hand, I have been steered into the arms of a beautiful, eighteen-years-older woman and garnered my fifteen minutes of celebrity status by hiking the 2,174-mile Appalachian Trail from one end to the other. There have been victories and climaxes of ecstasy I never anticipated someone like me could experience.

We have a popular expression in the autistic community. When you have met one person with autism . . . you have met *one* person with autism. And most of us do have the potential to make outstanding contributions to society when presented with the right opportunities. Therefore, my tale is just one example of what can happen when there are enough people in a community to give someone like me a chance. Before you proceed, be forewarned: This is not your *typical* book about autism. You, the reader, will get a taste of the good, the bad, and the downright weird. Have a good time!

FIRST IMPRESSIONS

My family lives in a neighborhood prone to the solicitations of kindhearted but uninvited visitors, many of whom are Jehovah's Witnesses. Dismissing unexpected visitors is always difficult for me because of the Asperger's syndrome as well as my general belief that even the simplest dilemma has to be resolved by making everything as complicated and unnecessary as possible. Only three options come to mind.

The first option is to turn the welcome mat into a spring-operated catapult that flings my unwanted visitors into the treetops with medieval force. My victims would bounce from branch to branch like pinballs before safely landing with cartoonish precision. The second option entails carving a massive square in my family's doorstep and hollowing out a cavernous lair beneath our front yard. After scavenging the darkest corners of the earth,

I'll stock my dungeon with monstrous beasts thought to be either mythological or long extinct. Most of the creatures will be unclassified raptors from the Cretaceous era. Although a handful will be soulless, hulking green trolls expelling boiling acid from a slanted orifice in the forehead. They shall harmoniously coexist while sharing an insatiable hunger for human flesh. The feedings will transpire within seconds and litter my *Land of the Lost*–style labyrinth with the skeletal remains of doomed solicitors still clutching their literature.

The third option seems more sensible. But, in my opinion, it is just as cruel and unrealistic. The third option is not answering the door and hiding from the Jehovah's Witnesses as if they were the gestapo. Plenty of non-Asperger's individuals would cower out of sight until the doorbell stopped blaring. But I have never believed in using "ignoring" as a means of relaying a message unless every other option has been exhausted. People, regardless of whether they have a social disability, just want to be acknowledged. Which brings me to a fourth option: *just answering the door and being honest.*

I open the door with absolutely no regard to my physical appearance and exaggerate this apathy by intentionally greeting visitors in my bathrobe. My privates could easily be exposed, but no one ever has the *cajones* to mention it.

The smiling man hands me a religious pamphlet and says, "We would like to give you this on behalf of our church."

To which I then reply, "I'm really sorry, but I don't want it and will probably throw it in the garbage five seconds after you leave. You should give it to someone who will actually bother to read it."

The man reacts like a gentleman. "I understand, sir. Have a good day." Through the veil of politeness, I can see he is offended and automatically judges me as an asshole. If only he understood why I refused to take his religious paraphernalia. And it has absolutely nothing to do with my resistance to joining his religion (though I could never belong to any faith that prohibits the observation of Halloween, a holiday I celebrate with obsessive enthusiasm). Ten seconds after closing the door, that pamphlet *would* make a beeline for the garbage and haunt me all day long.

Millions of these Jehovah's Witnesses pamphlets are churned out every year inside some tireless paper mill somewhere. And realistically speaking, 98 percent are rushed to the garbage with annoyed indifference because most Americans are too set in their ways to adopt an esoteric religion. Or they are too ravaged by twenty-first-century economic realities to invite additional change. These religious pamphlets always meet the same fate as the other solicitations imposing themselves in my mailbox. Sometimes I'm tempted to write a $20 check to the Save the Lemur Foundation or the Alliance of Bipolar Lubavitcher Rabbis, in exchange for return address labels with grotesque abbreviations for "Drive" and "Valley." But experience has taught me to do otherwise, because for every not-for-profit I make a contribution toward . . . ten more are going to show up within a month. The only not-for-profit foundations who do not dare ask me for money are the New York Blood Center and the American Red Cross. Considering I allow them to hook me up to phlebotomy machines once every two months, they are wise not to push the envelope (so to speak). My reluctance to make these contributions comes from the carnage of what was once a living tree.

Years before "going green" was in vogue, I was obsessed with recycling and maintained a phobia of unnecessary waste. When I fail to notice the cashier bagging my purchases, I'll remove them from the bag and carry them out by the armful. In college,

I chose to ri   ain.
The cup's lif   ime
as coffee bea   wn.
I finally bou   re-
fills eroded   nds
with third-d   ob-
lems in colle

My bruta   hen
compared t   tro-
typical is m   has
given to ind   The
other option   uld
make me . . .   tro-
typical and   ure

to appreciate each other's assets. My bitterness toward the neurotypical public derives from a lifetime of consistent rejections and lack of chances. Their contempt for me comes from misjudging the AS as a character flaw to be corrected. Regardless of how benign the imposition may be, it is also easy for neurotypicals to feel controlled and to push away. We push *so* hard against each other, like identical magnetic poles, and when a problem is finally addressed, it's sadly often too late to rectify the situation. For the most part, we are two opposing species drowning in our respective egos and judging each other on misunderstandings. No side is better or worse than the other. Just different . . .

Neurotypicals have a tendency to confront problems only *after* they have grown out of hand. Cyberbullying? It wouldn't have taken a carnival clairvoyant to anticipate the problem, but instead it took several well-publicized suicides for lawmakers to finally address what could have been avoided from day one. For all our deficiencies and challenges, people with Asperger's have at least one lesson to teach the population at large: Many problems can be resolved and even avoided altogether by just being a little more honest and direct.

On occasion, I actually find myself nostalgic for those childhood years when peers communicated with brutal honesty in response to my social ineptitude. It seemed like the lesser of many evils when compared to adult mind games and hidden signals.

Loser, Weird, Creepy, Geek, Stupid, Annoying . . .

I morbidly craved this type of attention because it was more gratifying than the alternative—being ignored. My childhood tormentors have finally matured into adults inhabiting the other extreme. Those adults who would have peppered me with cruel insults thirteen years ago now find it difficult to be honest with me.

Perhaps they are justified in their discomfort because, after all, there is no *kind way* to reject someone. Trying to reject someone without hurting his or her feelings is equivalent to loudly expelling flatulence in an Orthodox synagogue without offending its guests. (According to Jewish folklore, some Orthodox synagogues are so sacred the entire congregation must vacate the holy premises whenever someone farts.) Rejection is never kind, and even the most gingerly choreographed words never assuage all the pain. A saccharine rejection is just a sweet way of saying, "You are not good enough for me." Schoolgirls used to reject me by sticking a finger in their mouth in a mock attempt to induce vomiting. Now their adult reincarnations just smile at me in public and screen my phone calls after belatedly realizing that giving me their cell phone number was a mistake. They assume I'll get the message or will be sensible enough to give up. But the implicit message rarely comes with ease . . .

"I would think eventually you would take a hint! You are relentless!"

It is mystifying and maddening to watch neurotypicals communicate by . . . not communicating. The modern innovations of Caller ID and answering machines make it easier for the public to avoid those with whom they do not wish to cultivate a relationship. People who choose this tactic rarely do so out of malice, however. The neurotypical public chooses to "ignore" because it feels better than confronting a problem or worrying about hurting someone's feelings. But most individuals (Asperger's and neurotypicals alike) fare much better with closure. We all just want to be acknowledged . . . don't we?

Telemarketers are somewhat of a stretch, however. Whenever Caller ID flashes its digital warnings, it reminds me I have the liberty not to pick up the phone. Ignoring the phone call or promptly hanging up makes me a *hyppocwit*. Doesn't it? But allowing them to lure me into conversation is a waste of my time and theirs. It also increases the danger of giving someone my MasterCard numbers and being charged $100 to take a fake test for an obscure government job. (This has happened before on at least one occasion.)

Like someone afflicted with Asperger's syndrome, a persistent telemarketer may not get the message that someone is deliberately avoiding his or her phone solicitations. Maybe the potential customer is on a prolonged vacation. Or perhaps the customer returned from a New Age seminar and is now manically running town errands to overcompensate for a life of idleness. The Telemarketer Dilemma created an ethical crisis, and my solution was found in the most unlikely of settings: Spencer Gifts.

Among the erotic massage lotions, retro lava lamps, inflatable furniture, and classic gags (whoopee cushions, hand buzzers, etc.), I found a very practical device—the Gotta-Go Machine. This gadget has proven to be a handy tool for those telemarketers who just won't take "No, thank you" for an answer.

The Gotta-Go Machine is a pocket-size, plastic rectangle decorated with ten yellow, oval-shaped buttons. Each key emits a recorded sound, which allows me to remove myself from the conversation without being rude to a stranger trying to carve out a living, or wasting too much of our time. I have the following choices: another phone ringing, the doorbell, a crying baby, phone static, a dog barking, traffic, a siren, the smoke alarm, an overbearing wife calling, and an overbearing husband calling. The sounds are shockingly realistic except for the human voices, which are obviously digital forgeries. A victimless bit of fiction followed by an abrupt end to any phone solicitor's call.

When the next flock of Jehovah's Witnesses paid me a visit, it was necessary to dismiss them in the most unorthodox, complicated way imaginable. This time it was a cherubic, heavyset woman who struggled out of her car accompanied by a much thinner lady. As the former slogged her way to my front door, I felt disarmed by her theological benevolence, although it was not enough to keep me from enforcing my bizarre value system: *Paper Over Politeness*.

"Excuse me, sir? Our church would like you to have this pamphlet. Our mission is to spread the messages of Jehovah and we have a meeting next Saturday at our church."

I plaster the same sympathetic expression that my former

supervisor had on her face when she called me into her office to tell me I was being terminated from my group home job. I also filter out wisecracks trying to force their way through my mouth like verbal sewage. ("I'll attend your next Jehovah's Witness meeting if I witness this guy, Jehovah, miraculously finding me an online date this weekend who won't cancel!") But my honesty is appreciated, while simultaneously showing the woman I'm not merely being a jerk.

After I politely decline the first pamphlet, the thin woman pulls out a second one with ninja-like reflexes. "Do you have any children under age fourteen in your household? We have an incredible booklet about peer pressure." Upon examining the second pamphlet, I actually experience a fleeting moment of cathartic interest. It shows an anguished Jehovah's Witness boy dressed in church clothes who appears to be inside a school classroom. He is also surrounded by a jungle of his classmates extending their index fingers in his direction like poison-tipped arrows. The teacher is nowhere in the picture and could be ignoring the prepubescent wolves for all I know. She is tired of protecting a child who "chooses" to wear a suit and tie every single day . . . inviting such torment while making no effort to conform. Deep down, she believes he is doomed and must let nature take its course. But I reject this pamphlet, too.

"There are absolutely no children under age fourteen in my house. I am really sorry, ma'am. But I do not think I'll be able to come to your meeting, and it is not a good idea for me to take any of your pamphlets. You see, my family is Jewish, and we barely have enough motivation to go to synagogue anymore. So I do not think we're capable of committing to a new religion, and chances are your pamphlet is going to get thrown away. I would recycle it, but I'm not sure this paper is recyclable. It could end up in that swirling blob of garbage in the Pacific Ocean that is twice the size of Texas. You know . . . the one featured on *Oprah* two months ago? And this will cause me to obsess all day long because thanks to my Jewish upbringing I tend to feel guilty over the silliest things. I hope you understand."

By the end of my monologue, the woman's large hands, similar to Kathy Bates's in *Misery*, are covering her mouth while her body shakes with suppressed giggles. My family's overly nourished cat Jimmy is intrigued by the strangers and makes a shy cameo.

"Oh, is that your cat?" the thinner of the two asks. "Wow! He is very big!"

"Yes! And innocuous nonetheless!" I squeal. A question rises to my lips, although I'm not sure if it would be offensive: "Is Jehovah the same as our *God*? Or is it just a synonym for Jesus? Speaking of Jesus, I never knew Jesus Christ was a real person growing up and was afraid I would get in trouble for saying his name. I once had this uncle who always said, 'Jesus Christ!' in anger. So I instinctively assumed Jesus Christ was a synonym for an obscenity."

But common sense tells me I have pushed the envelope far enough for one day.

THE CARDS WE ARE DEALT

I've always wondered about the Comic Book Guy from *The Simpsons*. Besides being grossly obese and antisocial . . . I cannot help wondering whether he also has Asperger's syndrome on his plate. If you type "Asperger's" and "Comic Book Guy" on Google . . . you will be bombarded with links verifying the possibility. He is, after all, the tragic archetype of an individual with AS who still lives with his parents despite being in his mid-forties. The happiness most people would derive from social relationships is garnered from inanimate action figures preserved in their original display cases. He blurts out inappropriate criticisms regardless of the setting or possible dangers to himself. Inside a crowded bar, he gripes, "Beer is the nectar of the nitwit!"

Comic Book Guy also refuses to let go of his youthful diversions long after his peers permitted their mothers to give away those Vulcan ears and that stack of Spider-Man comic books. He was unable to parlay his stereotyped interests into becoming the next Steven Spielberg and justify his "weirdness." He is instead a tragic example of what happens when special interests rage like wildfire. They may even branch off into more destructive venues like World of Warcraft gaming addictions or obsessive hoarding. But a typical Asperger's individual needs his special interests almost as much as he needs social connections. Without hobbies and controlled obsessions to buffer the spurts of loneliness, suicide may seem like a sensible alternative.

My special interests have had the ability to both imprison and sustain me. They monopolize time that should be delegated toward friendships, employment, and other adult priorities. On the other hand, they have given me a predictable stability that I often haven't been able to find elsewhere. They have also contributed drama and passion to my life. Although no special interest has given me more ecstasy and agony than my short-lived blackjack obsession.

Gambling titillated me long before I surpassed the legal age of twenty-one. Even mediocre movies like Chevy Chase's *Vegas Vacation* were tolerable if they featured the exhilaration of casino gaming. The protagonists often lost their shirts, but in my eyes they were titanic heroes for taking such a risk.

When my father took me to an Upstate New York casino for the first time, he gave me $200 of his money and said, "If you win . . . keep your winnings and give me back my money. And if you lose it . . . you lose it." We were foolish enough to start at a table where the minimum bet was $25 per hand. After twenty minutes had lapsed . . . the two $100 bills had fallen through my fingers like talc powder. But the thrill of winning two out of the ten hands was enough to lure me to the ATM to withdraw $200 of my own money. The cash I had earned over two days of grueling labor at my IBM job was vaporized in a microsecond for the sake of a cheap thrill. This should have been enough to teach me a cruel lesson, but all I could think about was my next visit to the casino. My first taste of the blackjack tables locked me into a battle to escape from the Gambler's Hole regardless of how long it took . . . or how much money was wasted.

I returned to my room, where they probably pump oxygen to keep gamblers awake so they will return to the tables, only to lose more money or give back their winnings to the house.

Father says, "You seem to be a little shaken up. This pill will help you sleep." Then he adds, "There are people who have lost more than $200 on a single hand. And look around you, Jesse. Why do you think casinos are so lavish? People *lose!*"

My college, Hobart and William Smith, was only one hour away from the casino in Verona, New York, so I would make the drive every other weekend. I liked how blackjack was more complex than trying to get as close to the number twenty-one without going over. The human dealer becomes a machine possessed with benevolence or malevolent sentience depending on how the deck is stacked. A dealer is forced to continue hitting up to sixteen, but must stand on seventeen or above. The players, however, have the ability to conspire and strategize against this common foe. Together, we must turn the tables on the house and take advantage of the dealer's inability to deviate from the rules. A camaraderie soon develops among a table of extremely dissimilar individuals who do not judge me on my Asperger's mannerisms. On the left of me may be Andy—a successful lawyer with two very young children. Sitting on the right is Phil, who became a grandfather at age forty after a life of consecutive misfortunes.

"Yeah, my stupid daughter got herself pregnant when she was sixteen while having sex with my wife's new husband. I warned her this would happen if she were not careful. But the father of my grandchild is now in jail for selling drugs. And the judge gave him a few more years for screwin' my daughter!"

I cannot decide whether to say something comforting or make an obnoxious wisecrack. I settle on the most neutral thing I can think of in fifteen seconds.

"Yeah . . . that'll do it, I suppose."

The wisest adage I have ever heard about gambling came from an eighteen-year-old acquaintance who had never been to a casino. He warned me, "Any money you choose to gamble with is money that you should expect to lose. You are just doing it for entertainment." Blackjack quickly proved to be a lose-lose proposition, but the casino's "breaks" were still more magnanimous than real life. When Phil and I had a good day at the casino, we felt like winners in life. Sometimes even heroes, when our risky decisions kept the entire table from collectively losing hundreds of dollars. Furthermore, we lived for the visits that let us siphon self-esteem when it took too much effort to look in the mirror and give to ourselves what was just not coming from reality: *You are a winner . . . You are doing the best you can with your situation . . . Your luck will eventually change.* Being a winner only 20 percent of the time was far better than feeling like a loser 100 percent of the time.

You cannot turn left or right without viewing at least one of those signs inscribed, "For most . . . gambling is a fun activity. For others it is a serious problem. Know your limit and call 1 (800) 999-9999 for help." This ridiculous sign makes as much sense as D.A.R.E. pamphlets in a crack house. A person would probably not reach their epiphany in a House of Vice. Clarity comes when the electric company shuts off the power or a person suffers the public humiliation of watching the grocery store cashier cut up his MasterCard.

Gone are the quasi-nostalgic days of yore when casinos were seedy lairs lined with gnarled cigarette butts smoked down to the filter. Or guarded by menacing henchmen ready to drive gambling cheats into the middle of a secluded desert. These days, all casinos are hybrids of a Venice Beach mall and a local Holiday Inn. It is difficult not to be seduced by their man-made waterfalls gushing into lagoons of shimmering change reflecting the wishes of many thousands of beleaguered souls. All casinos are a composite of the Emerald City and the Ivory Tower of *Fantasia*. The glass ceilings, rainbow-colored carpeting, and engineered lighting are always radiating with the possibility of immediate wealth, gratification, and power . . .

One of these days, I am going to open the first gaming establishment to specifically cater to the Asperger's population. The socially downtrodden would come to my House of Cards not just to escape their realities, but to find the courage to face their obstacles. At least 40 percent of the dealers and other staff shall have AS, too. The ambience will be a quirky cross between *Pee-wee's Playhouse* and the quintessential Magical Land of Oz for Star Trekkies.

Visitors to my gambling mecca would be greeted by sprawling neon letters bearing the title, "Asperger's Land" or "The Wonderful Asp" (a slight take on a lyric from REM's "Man on the Moon"). Mine shall be the progressive sort of casino that values social responsibility, as staff liaisons keep their eyes open for lost souls gambling themselves into financial ruin. Either I or one of the softhearted staff will put our arm around that individual and gingerly whisper, "Sir, maybe you have gambled enough for one night. I would like to give you a free ticket to the trampoline room!" We will both then be startled by the shrieking sound of a toy train—one of thirty locomotives circulating a labyrinth of tracks suspended five feet above the card tables. The perpetual railroad traffic will be arranged with scientific precision, with plumes of actual smoke expelled from dime-size orifices.

Different rooms will cater to different obsessions, such as a room devoted to Disney paraphernalia, another crammed with 1980s memorabilia, and guests will enter their rooms to find bouncy balls on their pillows instead of the standard chocolate mint.

Until this fantasy comes to fruition someday, it is impossible to sugarcoat the brutal realities of gambling that will never "back off." *Especially* for someone with a social disability.

There are definitely times when a king and ace will unite like a psychedelic kaleidoscope as I clasp my hands in relief. Only once in a while will I swagger out of the casino with $200 more than was originally in my pockets. This sensation of winning always makes me feel on top of the world—but only for a short time. As soon as I return home, the wad of cash is carved into slivers with a lubricated pizza slicer. The slivers are then diced into a thousand tiny particles, which instantaneously diffuse into various facets of my life. They are eaten alive by car payments, credit card bills, postage stamps, a few used DVDs, and the mandatory breakfasts at the Daily Planet restaurant. My $200 surplus dissolves like it never existed in the first place, while making only half-moon indentations on my life's expenses. On the other hand, a loss of $200 conjures up different emotions, as I obsessively calculate the bills and frivolities that could have benefited from the squandered cash. It is money that would have, could have, and should have been invested in my special interests. The Disney classics, jack-o'-lantern carving materials, potentially doomed online dates, birthday cards, and postage. The loss of $200 gouges out a festering mental wound that takes at least two weeks to heal.

I haven't returned to the Gambling Mecca since the time I walked out slapping myself in rage . . . oblivious to the stares of bystanders. My innate persistence usually proves to be fatal when I remain at tables where I've lost nine times in a row and pushed once. Statistically and spiritually, I feel entitled to a reverse in fortune or fear the next table will be even worse. Therefore, I linger in this bad situation even as tears of bitterness well up in my corneas. I've barely suppressed the impulse to intentionally spill my lukewarm beverage in a childish act of passive-aggressive defiance. Coffee and diluted Sweet'N Low shall coat the table while provoking a chorus of groans. But the Deck of Malice will be destroyed as my losing streak comes to an abrupt halt. I also fear my frustrations could someday brim to a climax, with the dealer serving as the most convenient target for my displaced anger. I'll unleash a tirade of dormant rage and accuse her of not shuffling the cards correctly. Either stunt will earn me an armed security escort as well as a "little talk" in a private room. It will create additional trauma to be remembered by the body forever . . . revived by the aroma of cigarette smoke. Or even the Astroturf texture of a billiards table.

Someday I will return to the fantastical glitz of a casino, when losing $200 does not seem like such a big deal. Most important, my self-esteem will not be dependent on the sequence of those damn cards. I'll play the game when I'm more mature and capable of handling the inevitable losses. After all, the game did give me excitement while serving as a metaphor for life.

Sometimes the dealer will throw me two eights like ninja stars. The eights remind me of two curled serpents because they equal sixteen—the most loathed hand in the game of blackjack. When a player "hits" on sixteen, there is a decent chance he or she will go bust. And if the player "stands," then the dealer could just as easily brandish a seventeen or higher. But two identical cards make it possible for a player to "split" them into two separate hands, which are played out with nervous anticipation. A sixteen can easily be changed into two eighteens or better. After all, we do not always have control over the cards we are dealt. Just how we play the hand. And my obsessions could either help me reach for the stars or ground me deeper into a living hell.

I would finally realize my blackjack obsession was purloining too much money from other venues that could create real happiness for myself and others. The money that used to be pissed away at the blackjack tables was invested last Halloween on a $95 Beetlejuice costume and realistic-looking nunchucks, which had an impact on the neighborhood children that lingered far longer than a good day at the casino. It is ironic how the obsessions and perseveration synonymous with Asperger's syndrome was responsible for halting a more harmful, financially devastating obsession.

Like blackjack, the majority of my special interests have been intense but fleeting. I've also maintained absolutely no interest in turning my childhood room into a time capsule for action figures and comic books. In 1992, I purchased the #75 "Death of Superman" comic, in which he sustains mortal wounds from a monster named Doomsday . . . only to find it had compounded a pitiful $17 after I'd hoarded it in my room for nearly two decades. I do not share the same stereotypical interests as many of my peers, but have flirted with the tragic Asperger's stereotype on many occasions. While vigorously swinging my red-and-blue nunchucks in the living room last October, I came to a disturbing assessment of my life and feared someday reaching the same desperation as Comic Book Guy. Even more frightening was the realization that I was one year younger than the infantile loser in *Freddy Got Fingered*. But in the end, I know better than to entertain such fears when so many victories have been enjoyed in the past.

If all else fails, I'll always have YouTube, which is the ultimate Asperger's utopia. People with too much free time on their hands consistently post gold nuggets of near-obsolete nostalgia, as though sending a wink through the secret channels of the Asperger's community. It is an open faucet of digital stimulation, and unlike the blackjack tables . . . it is free. Most recently, I enjoyed the 1967 television special *Jack and the Beanstalk* with Gene Kelly and Hanna-Barbera animation. The blend of live action and animation was magical and neutralized any temptation to return to the blackjack tables. No matter what my life's realities happen to be, I'll always find something to assuage the pain until the most important cards turn in my favor.

CAT-SHIT FANTASIES AND HOLIDAY GREETINGS

With every job that must be done, there is an element of fun.
You find the fun and . . . *snap!* The job's a game!

—MARY POPPINS

As the only male child in our household, I automatically inherited the chores no one else wanted to deal with—chasing skunks out of the yard, garbage maintenance, and other unpleasant duties. The tasks became progressively more repulsive as I approached young adulthood. When two cats were welcomed into our household, I was promptly put in charge of what my father called Turd Maintenance.

Shifting through grainy cat litter for fecal deposits and solidified urine became less disgusting when I pretended to be a Sierra Nevada prospector during the California gold rush of 1848. The clumps of cat excrement were actually gold nuggets to finance my corrupt rise to power in the Sacremento legislature.

I also insisted on filling up the same garbage bag over a period of two months. Tiny increments were added day by day as I contemplated how so much matter could come from creatures so small. My father uneuphemistically coined it "The Big Bag of Cat Shit," and it greeted my family several times a day by the garage door. When he kept pestering me about when it would be thrown away, I looked at my father in confusion. Why would I throw away a garbage bag only half-full? The other garbage bags were never disposed of until their volumes had been depleted, and to do otherwise seemed like a wasteful act. But the shit will inevitably hit the fan sooner or later. Only it is not always the fan . . .

It happened one July afternoon as I was staring out the window watching a squirrel break open the impenetrable casing of an acorn. The screams coming from the garage were so intense even the squirrel dropped its acorn and made a nimble retreat into the branches.

"OHHHH, GOD! HE FILLED THAT FUCKING BAG TO THE TOP!"

The outburst was accompanied by alien chuckles of sympathy and bewilderment. It took only half a second to realize what had happened. My parents were leading friends through the garage and had made a hasty attempt to remove The Bag before having to concoct an explanation of why the Saperstein family liked to hoard a massive collection of cat excrement. Its elastic fibers, weakened by sixty days of moisture and fine abrasions, could no longer sustain its contents. Scruffy and Tiger's "leavings" flooded the front of the garage while burying my father in feline feces up to his heels! For some reason, I was never punished for these antics, and nobody even forced me to clean up the mess. My parents did not usually enforce punishment, in favor of conserving their energy to better understand their enigmatic son.

I often wonder how my parents survived my childhood without committing infanticide. How exactly did they maintain their sanity during years of erratic behavior; obsessive, time-consuming rituals; and what can only be described as a permanent "silly phase"? A few of these ritualistic obsessions have even persisted into adulthood.

As an eleven-year-old, I went through a prolonged phase in which I spoke almost entirely in rhyme, like an effeminate robot from some bastardized universe of Dr. Seuss.

"Hey, Jesse! Could you please take out the garbage before it gets dark?"

"Um, yes I could. I mean . . . that is one thing totally understood."

"Oh, God! Stop the gibberish, Jesse! It's enough already!"

"That's not very nice! And I happen to have a horrific case of lice."

(I would then proceed to scratch my itch-less head as if to validate the rhyme.)

My family has learned to tolerate my Asperger's demons, which are short in duration while squall-like in intensity. Every holiday season, they embrace the Perfect Storm of madness with lukewarm enthusiasm. Asperger's syndrome is a perpetual weather front. Sometimes severe . . . sometimes benign . . . but never, *ever* inert. The cyclone of weirdness, manic activity, and scramble to beat the clock always peak around Thanksgiving when I retrieve "The Box."

The Box is stored in my family's basement—a carpeted mausoleum of my childhood. The Box is also surrounded by flaking Halloween garments and warped wands shedding glitter from plastic stars. A storage closet houses the remains of a Super Nintendo Entertainment System, which has not seen an electrical outlet for more than a decade. For too many years, it pacified me with artificial self-esteem as I earned points and defeated nemeses in a virtual universe. It also stole hundreds of precious childhood hours that should have been devoted toward making friends or at least making more of an effort.

The Box is filled with unused Christmas cards, Yuletide-themed stamps, return address labels from not-for-profits, and holiday paraphernalia. Among other things, it holds a scratchy VHS cassette of the Claymation classic *Rudolph, the Red-Nosed Reindeer*, taped from the Disney Channel during the waning years of the Reagan administration. Its quality is scratchy, and the heavenly narration of Burl Ives is barely audible.

The Box's contents serve as a passive-aggressive monument for residual childhood bitterness. Throughout my childhood, I remained envious of my gentile peers who indulged in the commercial and familial beauty of Christmas as I chose to express my rage in inappropriate venues. On one occasion, I cried out "Merry Christmas!" instead of "Shabbat Shalom," and once I coerced the rabbi into letting me read my original "Chanukah Poem" in front of the packed congregation. Naturally, it would have been a courteous gesture to warn the rabbi that every single verse was modeled after "The Night Before Christmas." Someday I'll own my own house, which shall be mercilessly smothered with tacky lights, menorahs, and seven-foot-tall Santa figurines leering over an irritated neighborhood. The display will provoke a torrent of hate mail from angry Jews and Christians alike . . . as though this is the worst crime someone could inflict upon the human race. In the meantime, the best I can do is dive into The Box.

For days and nights on end, all I can do is write Christmas cards. A few Chanukah cards are composed here and there, but 90 percent is Noelish cheer. Bathing is often neglected in favor of giving the cards a four-day window to reach their destination.

Obsession, Noel, and Asperger's syndrome unite in a Royal Tripod of Weirdness. "Normal" people write the clichéd sentences everybody else includes: "I hope you and your family are enjoying the holiday season, and I look forward to seeing you after the New Year." But I write in my own language, which I call Aspergish (an extinct dialect of Anglo-Saxon Gibberish). Every space must be filled with handwritten ramblings as the card starts to overflow with an overbearing randomness. Furthermore, I show absolutely no consideration for the reader's comfort level and/or attention span:

As I write this card, I'm also watching a DVD of *The Pee-wee Herman Christmas Special*. It is allowing me to marinate in the simmering juices of nostalgic clay animation and modern Howdy Doody puppeteering. And thanks to the glorious vault of YouTube . . . this nostalgia is ever the more potent in adulthood. Things have been going well with my family this year. My sister, Dena, just brought home a stray cat named Jimmy, who is the quintessence of smallness. I hope you have a good holiday season and forge onward with the raging relentlessness of winter. My nickname for winter is "The Jewish Mother-in-Law Season." Because once it sets in, it is a real pain-in-the-butt to get rid of!

After remembering my obscure neighbors have two little boys around nine years old, I change my tone to an emasculated knight plotting his next conquest:

Mason . . . Sean . . . I look forward to the first blizzard so we may continue our snowball battles from last year. The legend shall rage forward and onward. I will destroy you!

Like many individuals with Asperger's, I am soothed by constant routine and repetitive motions. Fold, open, stuff . . . peel adhesive barrier strip . . . horizontally press, toss in pile . . . and repeat at least one hundred times. Is it tight enough? Did I put the right name and address on the cover letter? The den steadily evolves into a sea of return address labels; envelopes; cards; dried-up pens; and dead, distorted adhesive strips. The final garnish to my routine are those self-adhesive stamps that transform each inanimate letter into a white courier pigeon, with their ostentatious images of the Muppets, Disney characters, *Star Wars* icons, and other fantastical postage insignia. What could be more breathtaking?

And then there are my DVDs.

For a very long time, I resisted the temptation to purchase DVDs, considering how ridiculous it seemed to pay up to $24.99 for the same movie found on a VHS tape for at least half that price. But when I reluctantly purchased my first DVD, *28 Days Later* during my junior year of college, it instantaneously blossomed into another Asperger's obsession. There was just something about those glossy disks that drove me crazy with desire. I spent much of my free time aimlessly browsing the used-DVD aisles and would initiate conversations with store employees about their DVD-collecting strategies. I became part of a subculture preoccupied with accumulating as many DVDs as possible without going bankrupt. The Best Buy store became a digitally enhanced utopia where I could seize the original Disney masterpieces being defiled by pathetic, straight-to-DVD sequels (*Lady and the Tramp II, Cinderella II, Pocahontas II, The Fox and the Hound II, Return to Never-Never Land*, etc.). I eventually discovered the wonder of Amazon.com, which allowed me to buy DVDs for less than $10 apiece. It was not an expensive hobby, and my DVD collection quickly swelled. But tragedy struck upon returning home from my last year of college. I could not find my entire DVD collection!

For someone with Asperger's syndrome, losing the components of an obsession *is* the end of the world. Like a distressed Labrador searching for a lost bone, I rummaged through and tore apart every single box in my room. It became painfully obvious what had happened. The precious collection had either been snatched from my open car window during the chaos of packing or stolen from my dorm room. And I was in uncontrollable hysterics.

I ran through the house slapping the staircase wall and even hitting myself a couple of times. My neck muscles emitted a crackling snap like my grandfather's arthritic knees when rising from an orthopedic chair. For the next week I would pay a terrible price when the simple act of checking my blind spot while driving would produce sharp pain. My temper tantrum escalated as my parents frantically searched for the DVD collection. Nothing else could diffuse the escalating tantrum other than a possible fainting spell.

"God, Jesse! They're only things! Just things!" My father knew my reaction was exacerbated by my disability as well as a lack of life experience. Fortunately, the DVD collection was eventually found. They had been packed into an obscure box I never even thought of searching. Armageddon was just barely averted.

My obsessions have *superficially* melted through maturity, even though my reaction would be just as extreme if I now really did lose my DVD collection. But perhaps I would compromise by not hitting myself again or finding a more constructive outlet for my hysteria. "Maturity," after all, is just one of those buzzwords used to describe someone making an effort to compromise their destructive nonconformity.

I still make a manic effort to compose more than one hundred cards at least three business days before Christmas. It is *important*! My parents hardly condone this obsession, but are magnanimous enough to show halfhearted tolerance.

After doing the simple math, I am sporadically disgusted with myself. The season's greetings take about two weeks to prepare. Therefore, by the time I am fifty years old, I will have sacrificed more than one whole calendar year toward the cards. And perhaps one dark morning, I'll wake up as an angry middle-aged man who realizes he wasted a lot of time communicating with people who were probably laughing at him.

The most ominous clouds congregate within the Saperstein household when I begin sending cards to obscure acquaintances. Like the picturesque James family across the street . . .

"Jesse . . . *Jesse*! Knock it off already! Nobody sends three-page cards to people they hardly know. It makes them uncomfortable and you are *imposing* on their lives!"

I fire back, "First of all, my intentions are good and they must know I'm a nice person. Second of all, the great-grandmother lives next door, and I shovel her sidewalk for free when it snows. And third of all, I have earned the right to impose myself!"

Finally, the weeklong argument is settled with a compromise. I agree to mention my case of AS at the end of the card, while being generous enough to give my recipients a choice.

I hope your family enjoys the holiday season and you enjoyed my three-page card I wrote while watching "It's a Wonderful Life" subsequented by Bill Murray's "Scrooged." If you do not want to receive any more three-page cards then please give me the courtesy of letting me know. I am affected by the mildest form of autism known as Asperger's syndrome and these cards are how I choose to communicate with people.

In addition to the Christmas Card Obsession, I still store our cat's excrement and solidified urine for at least two months at a time. But I now keep The Bag in a secluded location, away from company. When The Bag reaches maximum capacity, I'll lovingly carry it to the garbage can, while supporting it from the bottom. In my mind, this obsessive behavior has yielded a planet-changing breakthrough. I have discovered that the methane properties of cat waste can be fermented into a clean-burning, renewable energy source that has eliminated our dependency on fossil fuel. Like Brazil, who processes sugarcane extract for energy, we are finally energy independent. Penetrating the Alaskan permafrost for petroleum and groveling to unstable Middle Eastern nations is no more than a shameful memory. We have ceased raping Mother Earth of her natural resources, while global warming has come to an abrupt halt. After all, the juice to power cars and fly airplanes is *all* derived from the residue of cat excrement.

The benefits of my scientific breakthrough have branched out into other sectors of society. Sprawling farms now breed millions of felines for the sole purpose of harvesting their waste. Families who would otherwise be in the throes of poverty are trading their cats' excrement in exchange for large government checks to carve out a cushy, middle-class life. It has created millions of new jobs in the private sector—my discovery has solved our energy problems as well as terminated the economic crisis two times over. President Barack Obama and I gleam as the Alfred Nobel medallion is placed around my neck as an artillery of flashbulbs lights up the Stockholm Concert Hall like celestial fireworks. Most important, I have transcended to the level of Asperger's Nirvana. I have reached that summit where my flamboyant weirdness is rewarded by national heroism and the Asperger's stigma is absolved forever.

In the meantime, I do not really mind if the local sanitation workers are left shaking their heads in disgust while asking, "What sort of family keeps a fifty-pound bag of cat shit in their house?"

EMPATHY: REAL, ARTIFICIAL, AND DIFFERENT

Like many children with Asperger's, I watched exorbitant amounts of television to buffer the chronic isolation. Too many hours of my childhood were spent watching family-oriented sitcoms including *Full House*, *The Simpsons*, and *Family Matters*. These shows revolved around an unstable family dynamic, and the formula was simple. Every episode focused on an outrageous conflict solved in the span of thirty minutes (not counting commercial interruptions, of course). These fictional personalities were also burdened with conspicuous shortcomings. For instance, *Family Matters'* Steve Urkel (Jaleel White) is a tenaciously annoying, socially inept nerd whose path of destruction is forever paved with good intentions. And worst of all is Homer Simpson—a fat, lazy, quasi-alcoholic slob who routinely strangles ten-year-old Bart in response to his shenanigans. Homer is also small-minded, politically incorrect, and fiscally irresponsible. I could list more of Homer Simpson's personality flaws, but my space is limited.

The personalities of our favorite characters never change. Their flaws remain the same, which is why we remain loyal viewers. What would have been the fate of *Married with Children* if Al Bundy had removed his hand from the vicinity of his scrotum to take charge of his sad, mediocre life? Or *Family Matters* if Steve Urkel had jettisoned his nerd persona forever to transform into a debonair and successful ladies' man? But once in a while, we see glimmers of hope and change. TV characters are capable of redemption, acts of heroism, and the most important quality that should define all human beings. *Empathy*. Even Homer Simpson rushed to the aide of his arch-nemesis, Ned Flanders, after his wife Maude died in a freak accident (an accident inadvertently caused by Homer, of course!).

A notable exception is *Seinfeld*, a show whose four main characters are selfish, egotistical, and shun self-improvement. For example, real people react differently when they witness an obese, defenseless man getting mugged. A brave few will jump in to help. Although most of us would rush into a store to call the police, because cemeteries are populated with heroes. The *Seinfeld* gang, however, chooses to videotape the incident while giggling at the poor man's anguish. Canned laughter aside, I have come to the conclusion that *Seinfeld* is a dank cesspool of humanity. It always makes me cringe because I am reminded of a negative stereotype of Asperger's syndrome that justifies intolerance. The neurotypical public feels entitled to condemn a population who appears to lack empathy or consideration for other human beings while trampling their boundaries like a bed of posies. Before some of my teachers even knew Asperger's syndrome existed, my uniqueness was judged as a black-and-white character flaw with no redeeming shades of gray.

In elementary school, we were graded on social conduct in conjunction with our class work. Did we share and play well with others? Therefore, my chances were similar to the proverbial ice sculpture within Dante's Inferno. My mother read the comments on my second-grade report card and responded in anger. In retrospect, perhaps it was more fear because her child lacked a critical human component. The criticisms were smeared with sterile, black ink: "Shows absolutely no consideration for others."

I could not understand why my mother was reacting so passionately as my father struggled to calm her down. "Every one of his report cards has something like this! Every single one since nursery school!" My father added, "Jesse, you had better learn how to care about people besides yourself!" It was a confusing evening because I did not understand what I had done wrong. Or how to fix it. My transgression was very simple. *I just did not care.*

I remember little Jennifer in my second-grade class. Later on, I would realize Jennifer was "special" and was the only child in my class with a hearing aid and severe speech impediment. One afternoon, poor Jennifer's hands slipped as she navigated the monkey bars . . . causing her to fall flat on her face. Shrieking wails provoked the attention of almost every student in my class as they rushed to her assistance. One resourceful child secured her detached glasses half-buried in a sea of alabaster pebbles.

"Hey! Give me her glasses! Don't crush her glasses."

I was there . . . but on the sidelines watching the commotion unfold, swelling with schadenfreude and amusement. Her wails sounded like a cow, and I stifled the urge to laugh at her anguish.

But her pain inspired an emotion within my classmates that has often seemed to me alien and artificial.

As an adult, I now offer my services to Asperger's students as an optimistic Ghost of Christmas Future. Perhaps listening to my experiences will save them from walking down at least one dark path and tripping over its fine crevices. But deep down I know better. They are going to make their own mistakes and will have to learn from the lingering consequences. The presentations are cathartic because maybe it would have made a difference if an AS adult had given me criticism that was actually constructive or fair, void of clichés such as "Stop trying so hard" and the worst, most ridiculous one of them all, *"Just be yourself..."*

I mentor a high school Asperger's class whose teacher is a beautiful redhead clone of Molly Ringwald. Over nearly three decades I have picked up social graces with slothlike efficiency, and barely have the common sense to avoid asking her out on a date. The woman, after all, is married with children. But my schoolboy crush makes conversation tenuous as I struggle to maintain professional decorum. The young man who interrupted our conversation had a suspicious grin and that should have been enough to deter me from falling into his trap.

"Hey, Jesse! Why don't you ask her about how her family is doing these days?"

She sighed while somehow remaining composed. "Actually, my two-year-old niece just strangled herself to death on the window blinds." Her voice was unflappable, as though used to the mordant outbursts of her students.

"My sister was only gone for a few minutes. It was just one of those days when someone called at the worst time. The crib was moved closer to the window that day for some reason. It was not even her regular nap time and my niece was wide awake..."

The boy continued smiling like a macabre figure from some Tim Burton fantasy. It was eerie he could be so oblivious. *So* complacent with the pain he had inflicted upon this poor woman. A gasp was stifled as my hand itched to slap this young man who had caused me such humiliation. Eventually, the anger waned as I realized how *hipochritical* it would be to put myself on a pedestal. The pain is more like cathartic, mental chemotherapy, inducing tumors prior to shrinking them. Repressed, bulbous tumors erupt along my torso and grow to a climax before the second round of chemotherapy kicks into action, drowning them in toxins. The malignant masses of negative energy usually recede when exposed to younger versions of what I used to be.

"Ryan died yesterday afternoon."

"Are you going to the funeral?"

I remember the October morning when melancholy zombies marched through the halls. Our seventh-grade class learned that Ryan would not be returning to school the next day after having been run over by a car. White plastic and electricity briefly sustained his broken body before he succumbed due to the extent of his injuries. He was a goofy but likeable kid whose only crime was crossing the wrong street, at the wrong time of day . . . with the wrong person behind the wheel. I looked down at my Nike sneakers, which were caked with mud and rainbow flecks of dead foliage. Mischief Night was coming in just a few weeks, but Ryan would not feel the adrenaline rush of running away from a police cruiser after some innocuous Halloween vandalism. Ryan also would never be carried off a baseball field before he and his teammates baptized their coach with Gatorade. But these unfair realities did not have the same emotional impact on me compared to those of my watery-eyed classmates.

A strange man entered my second-period science class, and I

took an immediate dislike toward him. He resembled a quasi-animated mannequin more than a severely inept grief counselor. Even with Asperger's syndrome, I was able to read his facial expressions and could tell he wanted to be somewhere else. He reminded me of a deformed puzzle piece not making the effort to fit into a foreign environment. My classmates were grieving in their respective ways. They shed tears, stared into space, looked confused, or lay their heads on the lab tables in shock. I chose to indifferently drum my fingers and was the only student who raised his hand.

"What kind of a car hit him?" I blurted out.

The entire class emitted a chorus of disgusted groans while the grief counselor ignored my ridiculous question. My lips parted to repeat the question because it seemed perfectly legitimate. After all, the details of the accident had to be discussed. What time did it occur? What was the velocity of the vehicle? Was the driver on medication or abusing some substance? What lessons can come out of this tragedy so that what happened to poor Ryan would not happen to us? Perhaps some Angel of Common Sense intervened to prevent me from pushing the envelope and demanding an answer. Not that day anyway . . .

The fine art of *artificial empathy* has been refined over the course of my adult life, as I have learned to function like a human computer. Like a cerebral Microsoft Word program, I have stored separate files for funerals, weddings, job interviews, first dates, etc. These files may be accessed at a moment's notice and compensate for my deficiencies with generalization—naturally understanding that the social conduct appropriate in one situation may be grossly inappropriate in another venue. Some situations produce more vulnerability toward the worst social blunders and require walking on eggshells. But they aren't typical eggshells. They are paper-thin robin's eggs laced with synthetic poison. Therefore, it is always critical to embrace new experiences because self-improvement is gained through flirting with disaster. This practice includes, but is hardly limited to, attending the funerals of obscure acquaintances. Or even total strangers if they are somehow connected to an obscure acquaintance. According to my skewed logic, the expression "Any friend of yours is a friend of mine" should apply even if this new "friend" happens to be dead and lying in a casket.

My mother solemnly handed me the *Poughkeepsie Journal's* obituary section one afternoon around my twenty-fifth birthday. The husband of a childhood occupational therapist of mine had died unexpectedly from a heart attack. My former therapist was kind, but our relationship died an immediate death after I stopped going to therapy fourteen years earlier. Of course, I never met her dead husband or had any emotional ties to him. These factors aside, it was time for Jesse's First Wake.

I walked into the House of Mourning and immediately modulated my monotone voice when approached by a former high school teacher. He had also never met the deceased and seemed to be trapped in the same awkward social bubble I was. Unlike me, however, I assume he was paying his respects because he and my ex-therapist worked for the same school district. I was in attendance to practice not screwing up during a more important funeral involving a close relative or friend.

"How is your life going these days, Jesse?"

I was about to begin a long-winded monologue about my publication aspirations, the post-apocalyptic world of online dating, my successful Appalachian Trail hike, and miscellaneous other subjects. But the Self-Control Data Program simultaneously began to download as my voice lowered to a near whisper.

I suggested to the teacher that we meet for lunch sometime, before turning my attention back to the corpse and his grieving family. Finally, I walked up to the open casket to view Jesse's First Dead Body. As the late George Carlin would say, "The man treated his body like a Temple. A Temple of Doom, that is!" He looked unnatural and was smeared with too much pancake makeup. I felt no emotion other than a nagging impulse to say exactly what was on my mind . . . letting it spill forth like a mouthful of toxic bile. I wanted to say:

> Hey, wouldn't it be funny if we pretended he is still alive like in that movie *Weekend at Bernies*? We could prop him up like a marionette and use strings to make him wave. But I doubt it would be possible in real life because don't dead people naturally stiffen up after death?

or

> It is kind of refreshing to see a man this fat lying down who is not just sleeping. Lots of overweight people have sleep apnea, and I cannot handle the sound of someone snoring due to my case of mild autism. If I were on an airplane and somebody were snoring, I would probably have to be escorted away by an air marshal or something. There should be a law against snoring because . . .

But an effort was made to be appropriate. I hugged my ex-therapist and said the standard "I am really sorry for your loss," without overdoing it. (I've learned that less is always more when it comes to funerals.) My "death dance" was flawlessly choreographed, even if the authentic empathy was missing. It was also excellent training for the future when I would actually work in a funeral home for a short time.

Empathy is defined as "feeling someone else's pain via emotional osmosis." Another person's anguish sends off vibrations, like a gunshot. These emotional vibrations do not always extend to me, unfortunately. As a college sophomore, I was not fazed when more than two thousand souls lost their lives on September 11. I spent the remainder of that Tuesday lying on a dock at Lake Seneca with morbid indifference. Also, I was grateful that my Sociology class had been canceled, while thinking about Ashley (the newest target of my romantic obsessions) and her compact blue car with a Pennsylvania license plate.

I sometimes wonder whether my diagnosis is just a bunch of bullshit, or clinical varnish for something much darker. Maybe Asperger's syndrome is a euphemism for being an unempathetic asshole who makes a deliberate effort to shirk societal norms. Is it a diagnosis to cower under, or an impervious umbrella that repels public criticism? Like the *Seinfeld* characters, I am someone who can provoke both ridicule and disgust. The shame sometimes grows so intense that I start to let people convince me that I deserve to be feared or hated. But most of the time I know better. Like autism, empathy is an enigma and manifests itself differently in each person.

My earliest memory of having something that I consider to be true empathy took place on the second day of sixth grade. My lunch money had been stolen out of my backpack, so I resigned myself to a day of semi-starvation until Edward (one of the weirdest kids in school and a fellow misfit) took pity on me. "I'll tell you what, Jesse," he said. "I'll lend you $1.50. Just pay me back tomorrow." I graciously accepted his offer.

Edward approached me the next day and gingerly asked for

the money back. I methodically dug into my pocket and handed him exactly $1.50. These actions seemed as natural as a sneeze, despite the fact that many teachers and classmates have viewed me as profoundly inconsiderate toward others. My father gruffly asked me later that day, "Did you pay that boy back, Jesse?" I nodded with a smile.

My encounter with Edward was the catalyst for a lifetime of what I experience as profound integrity and empathy. It did not take long to understand that failing to pay someone back would become the catalyst for feelings of shame and failure—emotions that would fester like a gaping hole carved by a mutant ground-hog into someone's manicured lawn. I had let someone down who trusted me. More important, their reactions would sear footprints of shame into my conscience while dredging up memories of my own bitterness. Their faces radiated with the same anguish I've endured when others betrayed me or took advantage of my fierce naiveté. In other words, I could sense their pain.

This vein of empathy became something to be sculpted and polished like a slab of marble. It became a form of overcompensation and a key to the elusive gates of neurotypical acceptance. In an amoral world where actions are often dictated by probable consequences or what is financially advantageous, it saddened me when my neurotypical peers did not always invest time to just take another look . . . They failed to give me credit for my fierce integrity—in my view, empathy, albeit with a lack of emotion.

People may wonder how someone who is so painfully self-conscious can lack an awareness of other people's pain. How can that guy be so smart, but have absolutely no common sense? How can someone appear so withdrawn, yet become so outgoing when he performs on a stage? It is easy for neurotypical people to get hung up on questions like these. But the reality is that there are no clear answers to the enigma of Asperger's syndrome, only unexpected treasures found once we make the choice to open ourselves up to the redeeming qualities of the AS population.

THE INABILITY TO LET GO

Like so much else, and as painful as it is, the bullying of the
past will have to be let go.

—MICHAEL JOHN CARLEY,
ASPERGER'S FROM THE INSIDE OUT

Like many victims of bullying, I have also played the role of bully
myself. Some of the taunting was directed at Scruffy and Tiger—
my family's sullen and indifferent cats. I loved flapping my hands
in front of their trigonometrically slanted faces, and they met my
nonsense with perplexed, gimlet-eyed stares. But the target of my
worst taunting was a five-year-old camper at Camp Hillcroft,
named Nathan. Nathan was only a year younger than me, but
the fact that he was unusually small for his age made him a walking dartboard for my taunts and insults. On the camp's lake-
shore, I would stalk Nathan while scaly reptilian heads peeked
up through the film of pond scum to witness the commotion.

"Oh, Nathan!" I shrieked while dancing around like a flip-
pant sprite. "You are as small as . . . a *little pebble*!" My fantasy
was to grab a tuft of his mane and hoist him off the ground like

an over-the-top villain from the surreal world of Roald Dahl. Poor Nathan made grunting noises while expelling loud sighs from his tiny lips . . . pretending not to hear me. I waited patiently for him to either burst into hysterical sobs or run away to find a camp counselor. But Nathan did neither. In fact, he possessed a granite courage that hyper-compensated for his tiny stature.

The day finally came when Nathan's annoyance brimmed to a climax. *Little* hands, coiled into *very small* claws, lunged toward my chest. He grasped the fleshy area around my nipples and rotated counterclockwise as though my bosom were two elastic faucets. I respected him for fighting back, although it was not enough to make me give up the intoxicating power. The afternoon arrived when Nathan finally acted on his threat to find his older brother. A much larger version of Nathan threw me on the ground a couple of times and towered above me like an eight-year-old giant. And my reign of day camp bullying came to an abrupt halt forever.

"There!" Nathan's brother thundered. "Now we're even!"

I do not condone bullying, but I can understand why it transpires within all schoolyards and camp lakefronts. Childhood is often synonymous with feelings of powerlessness. Our freedoms are severely limited by adults, and we are all vulnerable to being teased—some more so than others. When Nathan entered my life, I experienced a raw euphoria to finally hold such power over another human being. Ninety-nine percent of the time, however, *I* was the target of countless bullies who made most of my childhood miserable.

Sometimes the bullying I endured was nothing more than an innocuous rite of passage.

One afternoon my mother walked me over to a neighbor's house to play with three brothers close to my age. They were hiding in a tree house, and I scrambled up the first three rungs of its rope ladder. Like Nintendo games and vacations to the Jersey shore, a tree house was a rare childhood luxury. This one also housed a trove of toys, like a yellow plastic projector that played silent cartoons when you shoved a bulky cartridge in its chamber and turned a crank. From my sagging ladder rung, I eyed the cartridge that featured the Gummi Bears hurling boulders after drinking that cranberry juice potion. The brothers made it painfully obvious that my presence was unwanted as they guarded their domain like menacing fire ants. Finally, they came up with a task, and my reward for its completion would be access to their fortress. After a few moments' hesitation, I ran over to my mother and shyly extended my middle finger.

"Hey! That's not very nice," she gasped. I ran back to the brothers, who offered lukewarm praise for completing the task. Then they promptly handed me my next mission. I had to return to my mother and sing, "Kiss my dick . . . dance with my dick!" Fortunately, my mother's reaction to the first task was enough of an incentive to give up my fruitless efforts.

It was obvious the brothers were manipulating me for their own amusement, and it would be another few years before I understood "the middle finger" or the meaning of "dick." As if I were the protagonist of *Catch-22*, the boys would have continued raising my mission parameters. It made no difference how many lewd stunts were performed that afternoon, the glory of their tree house would always be denied. They were cognizant of their power and refused to show any mercy.

Only a few years later, the side effects of puberty combined with Asperger's transformed me into an aerobic Velcro pad for countless plagues of adolescence: acne, braces, an Elmer Fudd–like speech impediment, uncontrollable flatulence, clumsiness, a

learning disability, a comically oversized nose, a sonorous, monotone voice, and gullibility. I was spared no indignity and did not
receive many breaks during this period of extreme adolescent
anguish.

Like an incompetent anthropologist, I would lethargically
pick up the social graces relevant to each new environment during transitional periods. By the time I finally "got it," the damage
was usually irreversible because too many doomed first, second,
and fifteenth impressions had already transpired. Children also
have a natural talent for immediately identifying those peers who
cannot fit into the system. The most tenacious bullying surfaced
from age nine to fourteen, when it was not surprising to return
to my gym locker and discover my books had been merrily
thrown around the room like confetti. It was during this time
when a handful of my teachers seemed to condone the constant
bullying as a natural repercussion for being different. Two years
ago, I wrote a two-page article for my local newspaper about my
accomplishments and struggles with Asperger's syndrome. I received many positive responses from the Dutchess County community and one negative one.

I've taught middle school for over 30 years; I've also taught in-
clusion classes for 10 years with Asperger boys in each class,
each year. One of the reasons people "make fun" of these boys
is that most Asperger boys do not know their boundaries and
have trouble "fitting in" socially. One of the most pronounced
symptoms of their condition is boasting about themselves (because most of them are above-average IQ wise) and not realizing
the consequences. They also have very little tolerance for others,
especially others who don't understand or appreciate their accomplishments.

The gentleman who wrote me this email represented the viewpoints of a handful of teachers. But no educator was more malicious than Mr. Graham.

Mr. Graham was my fifth-grade teacher and a genuine asshole. Even my father recalls entering Mr. Graham's classroom as fumes of asshole-osity permeated his olfactory orifices like a rancid perfume. It was enough to overpower the more pleasant scent of chalk and Magic Markers. His room was also plastered with Mets memorabilia as opposed to motivational posters with free-falling skydivers and captions like, "A mind is like a parachute. It works best when open." One of his more bizarre posters literally insinuated that all Yankee fans were on drugs. My mother found it necessary to warn Mr. Graham of my history with bullying, to which he responded, "If any student is having social problems, it has been my experience that particular student is usually doing something to cause it himself." My mother had the common sense to have me transferred out of this class once he began sending me home with notes laced with snide remarks about my "stupid questions" and began singling me out in front of the class for being "the only child in fifth grade who still carries a *Beetlejuice* lunch box."

However, even Mr. Graham deserves the courtesy of a devil's advocate. It's possible his heart was in the right place and his contempt toward vulnerable children was merely "tough love." The schoolyard, it seems, is a dress rehearsal for the unfair realities of the adult world.

In seventh grade, it was common for someone to try to beat the living shit out of me as punishment for being "weird." My tormentors very rarely faced consequences, and the worst thing that could have happened to them was a weeklong suspension from school. The bully would have to endure five days of parental house arrest. He would be imprisoned among his collection of DVDs, Super Nintendo games, and other spoils. In the adult world, bullying may remanifest itself as a wolf in sheep's clothing through unfair job terminations, gingerly worded rejection letters, water cooler gossip, and party snubs. Furthermore, the consequences of "adult bullying" may extend to chronic unemployment, homelessness, and even suicide.

Only once in a while my problems were self-inflicted, as Mr. Graham insinuated, and sometimes it did serve as a barbed motivator to cease inappropriate behavior. During my preteen years, bullying encouraged me to stop touching myself inappropriately or endlessly probing my nasal passages for fossilized deposits. But most of the time, bullying was provoked by the same unjustified, irrational reasons it has always haunted the schoolyard. I was *different*.

Being different . . . being different . . . is being great!
It doesn't matter who you really are.
That's what makes a superstar!
Being different . . . being different . . . is being great!

This ridiculous jingle played for years on child-friendly networks like Nickelodeon while smiling children of all walks of life danced to the music. They looked unnaturally happy, as though their facial tissues had been injected with children's botox. Like Santa Claus or George W. Bush, it was merely saccharine, mythological bullshit. *Being different* transformed me into a walking "kick me" sign for bullies desperate to sate their hunger for power.

Teachers do not get much worse than Mr. Graham (The Asshole Incarnate), although several failed miserably as my advocates and protectors. They did what the neurotypical public often does when a problem arises. They ignored it in hopes it would eventually go away. Like Mr. Graham, they viewed bullying as a self-inflicted consequence of "choosing" not to conform. Maybe my teachers were even grateful for the bullies or viewed them as unfettered messengers for the discipline they could not legally dispense.

In reality, my teachers did not ignore bullying out of contempt for me, and my bitterness has melted over the years. They were adult men and women contending with aging and/or dying parents, mentally ill children, clinical depression, financial crisis, faculty politics, and other personal woes demanding constant attention. Advocating for me would sap time and energy that did not exist. Therefore, it seemed practical to avoid the problem in hopes it would soon die a natural death (like a fungus you pray will just wither away). And besides, the short-term effects of tackling the bullying could have easily spawned additional trouble.

The teacher would have been forced to listen to the extremely dissimilar sides of the story while devising a fair plan of action. The parental units might ultimately have declared war in defense of their respective offspring. They would threaten to take legal action against each other . . . the teacher . . . and the school. New problems would spread like a mass incubation of lice as the teacher juggled the other issues monopolizing his or her personal life.

Good intentions aside, it is dangerous to always condemn an Asperger's child for creating his or her own social nightmares. This form of tough love was responsible for an unhealthy, codependent relationship in which my self-esteem was at the mercy of my oppressors. Only sometimes did making the effort alleviate some of the teasing. For instance, in gym class I took competitive sports very seriously and harnessed my microscopic cache of athletic ability. I also drew inspiration from the fictional ten-page-long novella *Jewish Sports Heroes of the 20th Century*. My peers' genuine compliments coincided with each hollow smack inside my softball glove . . . every goal.

Making the effort can stimulate some social acceptance, although bullying will never be totally eradicated. Perhaps my unhappiness would have been less severe if teachers had explained the other reasons for chronic social failures. When people fail to understand *why* someone is different, they will often deny him or her the "radical" courtesy of *a chance*.

Few teachers prepared me for the rejections that would come crashing down like the moon-manipulated tides. Or the barren durations of hopelessness when I should have practiced staring into the mirror to germinate a sense of self that was not always going to come from my peers.

Rejection is still unbearable as an adult, and I have never stopped asking the same empty questions.

"What did I do?"

But victims are wise to consider the mind-set of a bully in order to preserve their own self-esteem. Plenty of bullies are victims of bullying themselves or have been scarred by worse abuse, such as domestic violence and molestation. They are vulnerable young beings grasping for celery-thin strands of confidence or anything at all.

Instead of building self-esteem through their accomplishments . . . it is easier to scour the schoolyard for easy targets. I'll always wonder why I did not make more of an attempt to fight back when people attempted to beat the living shit out of me. I probably would have lost, but maybe it would have made a profound difference to have landed just one punch. I'd experience the sensation of someone else's blood on my knuckles and know I'd inflicted deserved pain. Then I would accept the short-term consequences of school suspension or even police involvement if my retaliation went too far. Compared to the lingering demons of emasculation and anger, the former may have been the lesser of many evils. Like me on the Camp Hillcroft lakefront, my bullies were also cowards who would not have responded to reason and my teachers were anything but bodyguards. My suffering lasted longer than it should have.

Speaking of which . . .

I often wonder what could have happened if Nathan's older brother had not intervened at such an early age. Perhaps I would have graduated to weaker victims or served as a toady apprentice for the more menacing bullies. Bullying could have become the immediate gratification to replenish the void created by Asperger's syndrome. Assaulting one of my weaker peers might have ingratiated me into the league of bullying and warded off possible attackers. But thankfully, I veered away from this path during its infantile stages. It would not surprise me if Nathan is still haunted by our lakefront battles, especially if I was his first experience with bullying. As an adult, can he comprehend the extent of my cowardice and know he was actually the courageous one for fighting back? It is more important to be honest about my dark past than to risk turning into the fantastical Krit from the Land of the Hippos (gibberish for hypocrite). My adult act of contrition will be to counsel AS victims while battling bullying where it may proliferate. After all, I have never actually believed in *just letting things go* . . .

BAR MITZVAH MEMORIES

The eighth day of a Jewish boy's life is a harbinger of future misery. It will be a childhood of Hebrew school, Sunday school, confirmation, marathon synagogue services, Hebrew tutoring, tasteless unleavened bread for Passover, fasting on Yom Kippur, gefilte fish laced with horseradish, and alienation during a holiday season catered toward Gentiles (non-Jewish folk). But in terms of literal pain and suffering, these experiences are minor nuisances compared to a Jewish boy's bris.

I used to take baths until I finally realized how disgusting it was to sit in a stagnant pool of my own filth and urine. Once in a while, I would stare at my genitalia and assume they looked like their present state upon emerging from the womb. In reality, all human *schmeckles* (a Yiddish term) look like enchanted mushrooms wearing dunce caps prior to the act of circumcision.

The Jewish man who performs the bris is called a mohel (usually a venerable rabbi with decent eyesight and ideally unafflicted by Parkinson's-related tremors). While I have never actually seen the implement up close, I assume the tool of choice is a hybrid of a Lilliputian's sickle and those Biology class scalpels used to open chemically preserved frogs. The ritual is punctuated by bloodcurdling screams as spectators cringe in empathy.

While I'm certainly not suggesting we terminate a two-thousand-plus-year-old tradition, perhaps some progressive Jewish scholars will modify the bris for the twenty-first century. What would be so sacrilegious about rubbing a topical anesthetic on the penis? And in 1791, revolutionary France invented the guillotine as a humane method of execution compared to hangings or the breaking wheel. They believed the purpose of an execution should be to end life and not to exacerbate suffering. The same consideration should be given to Jewish boys, and I propose that we invent a Penis Guillotine to swiftly sever the foreskin. After all, I would imagine the act of removing the foreskin is prolonged, as the mohel tries to be precise in his sawing motions. This is the beauty of being a Reform Jew—the most lenient sect of Judaism. Not all of us keep kosher, and innovation is often tolerated.

I assume retired mob hit men are constantly looking over their shoulders. The children of their slain targets grew up a long time ago, but they can neither forgive nor forget. And it *was* personal! Therefore, I've always wondered whether mohels also have morbid nightmares related to their trade. In their dreams, are they the ones lying naked on their backs like immobile turtles in a roomful of strangers? His torso still belongs to a stocky, seventy-year-old Jewish man, but speech comes out like infantile war-

bling. The degrading whispers are very much audible: "Aww . . .
he has such a cute little penis!"

"It's either very cold in here or he is going to grow up buying
a lot of expensive cars!"

A much younger man brandishes a dull implement stained
with the blood of a previous circumcision. His smile is unusually
wide . . . much too vindictive. More young men, ranging from
age fourteen to thirty, join the circle with the same creepy smiles.
The mohel eventually realizes the converging guests have nothing to do with the family. They are just a handful of the hundreds
of infants circumcised throughout his *schmeckle*-slicing career.

My parents had the good intentions of assimilating into the Jewish community and pushed me to socialize with other Jewish
children. They enrolled me in Hebrew school at the start of third
grade, and admittedly took these actions out of concern for us
not fitting into the cookie-cutter mold of a "perfect" Jewish family. I guess my parents had an irrational fear of being ostracized
from the community, or believed everyone had nothing better to
talk about than why the little Saperstein boy did not attend Hebrew school. So many parents fall into this trap. Their child may
be maintaining a B average and is a star on the town soccer
league, but the Jones child down the street is an A student involved with soccer, football, and Boy Scouts, who takes private
jujitsu lessons on Saturday mornings. My parents rarely coerced
me into activities I despised with a passion or used me as a tool
to absolve their own regrets. However, they still insisted I have a
formal Jewish education.

Hebrew school met for two hours on Mondays and Wednesdays inside the local Jewish community center. That, combined with two more hours of Sunday school, was the equivalent of another full school day tacked onto the week. A typical third grader would have complained for a couple of weeks before grudgingly accepting this transition. But I grew progressively more miserable for the remainder of the year, until my mother came to her senses. She finally allowed me to drop out, and an Israeli woman tutored me once a week until my Bar Mitzvah. If this Hebrew school regimen had continued for four more years, chances are I would have concocted a stunt to get myself expelled. Maybe bringing a replica of Jesus on the cross and waving it around the classroom would have done the trick. Another possibility would have been carrying a roasted pig into the Yom Kippur feast (complete with an apple shoved in its mouth for aesthetic purposes). I'd sling it on top of a table, crushing the platter of kugel and gefilte fish. Jews are also prohibited from mixing dairy and meat, according to Talmudic law. That actually does make lots of sense. Chugging a glass of milk with a sirloin steak is repulsive, and my nickname for cheeseburgers is the "Ambrosia of Satan." But when Jews thousands of years ago would become ill from consuming shellfish and pork products, naturally, without the scientific knowledge of salmonella bacteria, they believed God was punishing them for eating this forbidden food. I've always mocked this as a vestigial superstition, particularly since my favorite delicacies are shrimp, clams, oysters, Maryland blue hard-shelled crabs, lobster, and glazed ham. Overall, my religious education was little more than a theological extension of my normal social isolation. And I usually referred to my family's synagogue as "The Temple of Doom" from the second Indiana Jones movie.

My mother and father did an incredible job offering me pos-

itive attention for the smallest accomplishments. Even if my lat-
est achievement was something as simple as taking out the
garbage on time or acing a Math test, they constantly made me
feel like a valuable component of the household. But it was never
enough to compensate for the social isolation provoking me to
seize attention through bizarre, sometimes dangerous, antics.
Anything to garner an audience and feel like the center of the
universe for a fleeting second.

I was rarely the kid who kicked the winning goal in a tight
soccer match, to be baptized into that fickle world of heroism
and non-homoerotic ass slaps. Nothing compensated for the
thirteen years of isolation subsequent to the partial amputation
of my penis, but a silver lining did exist at the end of a road
paved with anguish.

According to Judaic law, when a boy turns thirteen years old
he is officially a man. He is old enough to make a contribution
to the Jewish community while taking responsibility for his actions. The occasion is marked by a religious service and a subsequent mega-birthday celebration. A Bar Mitzvah can be a day of
profound joy, but it also has the potential to haunt you forever.

Although my Bar Mitzvah experience was less traumatic than
my father's, I despised everything about the ordeal: Hebrew
school, Sunday school, accruing the community service hours,
the Hebrew tutor, and the Bar Mitzvah tutor. One of my many
responsibilities included attending the Bar Mitzvah services of
total strangers. Every Saturday, I would wake up and pray another bastard would refrain from "ascending toward manhood"
as my imagination became the perfect buffer to the weekend's
suffering. It would be nice to have one of those rifles in the Steven Seagal action movies. Possibly the ones with the laser aiming
system.

When my rabbi spoke in front of my Bar Mitzvah class, he assured us, "You are going to be well prepared even if we have to postpone your Bar Mitzvah. Nobody is going to let you go up onto the bimah to make a fool of yourself!" My poor father was not nearly as fortunate. He was haphazardly tutored a few months prior to the event, whereas my Hebrew studies began five years earlier. Like a sheep goaded into the slaughterhouse, my father was prematurely forced onto the stage to recite Hebrew he did not know. The ordeal caused him to break out in hives around the crevices of his fingers.

Something would go wrong because I still hesitated instead of reciting the ancient calligraphy in my sleep. Perhaps I would puke on the Torah before the rabbi dragged me off the bimah with vacillating sentiments of rage and pity. I would go down in history as the only student in my synagogue who vomited on the holiest of scrolls. As we all know, performing in front of a crowd is nothing more than a flirtation with disaster. It is . . . isn't it? Trying to say the correct words? Dancing the right choreography and singing the precise timbre of song? Nothing more than an unnecessary risk as well as a charged liability. It seemed more sensible to sit down as an anonymous member of the audience.

I do not hear our beloved rabbi reading his portion of the Torah because I am freaking out. The synagogue president senses my fear and softly advises, "Just take a very deep breath." (Why do people always tell you to take a deep breath to combat panic? It never works and only leads to hyperventilation.) The rabbi scratches his long white beard like an emaciated version of Santa Claus. He is finished with his portion, and it is now time for me to take my place on the bimah.

The Hebrew poured out of my mouth with minimal hesitation, as the sea of gimlet-eyed spectators grew less intimidating. But, despite my years of preparation, I stumbled on a word in the middle of my Torah portion. The ancient word began with the "Cha" sound, but nothing was coming out except doglike panting. I felt the rabbi's gentle hand massaging my back, and as if this were a verbal Heimlich ... the word popped out. The rest of my performance went smoothly as "my universe" watched in admiration. I made absolutely no errors and thus eliminated any chance of criticism or shame. Even my cynical, cantankerous witch of a great-aunt had nothing negative to say all day.

The incredible day was not without its flaws, of course. A freak April snowstorm created hazardous travel conditions for the guests. Also, our caterer's hypothalamus could not process the task of copying down five letters, letter for letter. Lines of cake frosting displayed my name as "Jessie." Or was it "Jessy"? (To me this is not a minor error.) Last but not least, the band-leader never took the *radical initiative* of informing my parents he was not a people person and would not serve as the announcer like they expected. It is ironic how my father's Bar Mitzvah was responsible for his lifelong fear and hatred of public speaking. But his son's Bar Mitzvah was what caused him to overcome this phobia and rise to the occasion as the master of ceremonies.

My mother also seized the day to emerge from her shell. In front of my family and friends, she performed an original song in honor of my accomplishment.

The most important things in life are ones that can't be seen,
It's how you feel about yourself, your hopes and all your dreams ...

Don't be afraid to make mistakes,
Or change your course in life;
Follow your heart; let it lead the way.
That's the best way to go through life.

In my opinion, a bris is the ultimate test of one's manhood, and the act of circumcision should take place at age thirteen, instead of a Bar Mitzvah. After all, it takes a true man to let a stranger sever his foreskin in a public venue without so much as a whimper. Perhaps I would have even appreciated a teenage bris, based on how desperately I crave attention. Of course, I would squeeze someone's hand and make light of the situation with a few wisecracks.

"Hey! You be careful with that thing! Do not snip off anything I am going to eventually need on my wedding night!"

The Hallmark industry would also have a field day. I can just envision Lorena Bobbitt brandishing a butcher knife with the caption, "Guess who just got her mohel certification last week and is paying you a visit on your Big Day?" A Bar Mitzvah should transpire five years later, on a Jewish boy's eighteenth birthday, when he is officially considered an adult—mature enough to appreciate the experience without battling the pangs of adolescence. But for me, it was probably better the experience happened at age thirteen.

I took the "becoming a man thing" literally, without realizing it's just a bunch of metaphorical bullshit. It was hardly a barometer for instantaneous manhood, and not just because my first sexual encounter was eight years into the future. The fairy-tale magic of my Bar Mitzvah was terminated once my mother forced me to sit down to compose a mountain of thank-you cards. And on Monday morning, I returned to the jungle of seventh grade, where I was still vulnerable to the same bullying and isolation. The Bar Mitzvah solved none of my social problems, although the event became a critical turning point during a lonely childhood when no Asperger's diagnosis existed. It proved to be a catalyst for future victories, while encouraging me to "justify my weirdness" through talent and good deeds.

On my thirteenth birthday, positive attention morphed into an omnipresent force—radiating in all directions from family, friends, and obscure acquaintances. As is the custom, I was hoisted up in a wooden chair and thrust into an upside-down forest of streamers, animated neon lights from disco balls, and Mylar stars. The congratulatory din was overwhelming, addicting, and excruciatingly fleeting. My Bar Mitzvah eventually came to an end, just as everything in life always does. But it left me with an insatiable, lifelong desire to do it again . . . and again. More performances and social triumphs would follow. Furthermore, the "want" will always be strong enough to let me rise above my embedded fears.

MILLERTON DAYS

My father has this expression. "The sooner you decide to make friends with change . . . the easier your life will become." But for children with autism, change is a viscous poison known to provoke temper tantrums and distress. Abrupt deviations in my routine always felt like phantom limb syndrome for a recent amputee. I would reach down and immediately become distressed when a jarring absence replaced the comfortable insulation . . . that familiarity. With this in mind, my early childhood was stable and relatively free of earth-shattering changes. I also had one constant that made me feel safe until I approached early adulthood. Millerton.

My paternal grandparents lived only forty-five minutes down the road in a village called Millerton. For me and my younger cousins, Millerton was more than just a small town straddling the border of Connecticut. It was a portal into a Norman Rockwell painting . . . a time capsule for childhood innocence. I loved Millerton because very little ever changed within my grandparents' modest, white-as-a-picket-fence house. Millerton was my father's childhood home as well as my own boyhood haven.

Sometimes I was brave enough to walk through the pine forest to the edge of my grandparents' property. I never met their next-door neighbors, but became very familiar with their ominous black Labrador. As a six-year-old, I played a game in which I crept as close as possible, until the ebony beast came charging out of his dilapidated doghouse. He was constantly enraged and surely capable of leaping the fence to put an end to my cowardly games forever. It was clear that given the chance, this supernatural canine would shred my epidermis into fine ribbons without thinking twice. The barking became fainter until it finally stopped or I reached the safety of the white house. I played this game for what seemed like years . . . always trying to get as close as possible to the source of my terror.

Eventually the dog lost interest in my game. He became tired of constantly defending his domain and just seemed tired in general. The creature would make a brief cameo, look at me in disgust, and limp back into the shack. Eventually, he ceased making appearances even though the fence and doghouse remained intact. I assumed he had crawled back into his dwelling one hazy, summer afternoon and decided to hibernate for eternity.

The best part of Millerton was playing with my younger cousins, who seemed to naturally look up to me because I was the oldest. They believed what I said and did anything I told them. Sometimes the games were as harmless as gimlet-eyed kittens radiating innocuousness. There was the afternoon I grabbed ice cubes from the freezer and ran with my younger cousin, Tom, to the edge of our grandparents' sprawling backyard. We stopped by the pond that had once served as a watering hole for cattle during the Great Depression. I warned him about the cantankerous witch stalking the pond and ordered him to defeat her by throwing the ice cubes in her direction. Later that evening, the grown-ups listened to the ravings of a three-year-old who believed he had vanquished an evil witch with his older cousin.

Some of my other games were a bit more mischievous, and at times even dangerous. I recall the July afternoon I convinced my cousins to help me push my grandfather's riding lawn mower out of the garage. Fortunately, my aunt Sarah caught us before I had the chance to turn the ignition. Memories of my other antics cause me to cringe with shame. Like the afternoon I stole my grandfather's large magnifying glass to teach my cousins how to harness the power of the sun. The handful of dead leaves kindled on the steps leading toward the porch, but I still felt responsible because of the bucket of water by my side. Once again, my aunt Sarah caught us as I promptly doused my fire. She cried out, "You are very lucky it was me who caught you and not Grandpa." After he turned seventy, my grandfather lost most of his residual tolerance for childhood shenanigans. His body had also been weakened by a sinister procession of heart attacks, and perhaps the sight of a fire could have been the final straw.

My grandfather's chronic health problems and gruff demeanor often eclipsed one of his more endearing qualities. It was a personality trait rarely seen except in Freudian slips or stories passed down by elder generations of the Saperstein clan. Irving Saperstein possessed an unpredictable, often twisted, sense of humor. He loved walking into diners just to torment the waitresses. He would enter with his entourage and promptly announce, "We're from Canada!" as the waitress's expression plummeted in disgust. (Canadians are stereotyped as being infamously poor tippers.)

When my aunt Sarah was little, he once left the room to use a nearby bathroom. As my grandmother and Sarah watched television, he began loudly urinating. Two minutes passed as the sound continued. They began to look at each other in concern. "What is going on?" As one of his many pranks, he had connected a thin hose from the sink to the toilet!

The home of Irving and Shirley Saperstein resisted the constant innovations of the late twentieth century. While the grandparents of my peers were breaking down and purchasing Apple computers, the only quasi-modern amenity my grandfather allowed in his home was a remote control the size of a cinder block. Maybe I once caught a glimpse of the 1978 electronic game, Simon, lurking in some closet. (I doubt my generation even knows that Simon was the pioneer for every handheld video game over the next three decades.) Speaking of which, my younger cousins also brought their Super Nintendo Entertainment Systems and battery-operated gadgets to pollute the Grovers Corners ambience. These modern amenities stood out like anachronisms in a fiercely pathetic independent film—set in the 1950s. Change was kept to a tolerable bare minimum.

Then something terrible happened to nearly destroy Millerton for all of us.

Despite my social ineptitude and personality flaws, I rarely choose "ignoring" as a means of communication. But I do understand why the neurotypical public frequently relies on this technique when relaying a message. It is so much easier than expressing hard truths. It is easier than forming a gingerly worded rejection or confronting the awkwardness. As we all know, ignoring sometimes extends beyond social interaction. Tragically so, in some cases.

When my grandmother first noticed drops of blood on her underwear, she could have ignored these symptoms. Many people do. But she immediately made a doctor's appointment as she should have. Her uterine cancer turned out not to be as operable as we were first told. A few cells had already migrated to her stomach. And the unstoppable mitosis continued . . .

The rural house took on a malevolent appearance when a sign greeted me at the door: "No open flames, please! Oxygen tanks in use." Toward the end, my grandmother's bedroom grew into a jungle of hospital equipment and tubes. Corrosive chemotherapy turned this classy, proud woman into someone we no longer recognized . . . a skeletal figure in a perpetual state of suffering. I was transforming, too—from a relatively well-behaved kid into an unpredictable and inappropriate one. While my grandmother faded from our lives, my behavior was truly at its worst.

I grabbed my cousin Tom's package of Nickelodeon Slime and shoved it down my underwear. "OOOHHHH, baby!" I gushed as the cold, gelatinous substance hit my scrotum. "This feels so good!" Then I packed it into the plastic container and handed it back to Tom as though it were no big deal. Later that day, I acted upon another impulse and grabbed Tom's plastic tape recorder—the bulky, silver model made popular by *Home Alone 2*. An endless succession of profanities spewed into the microphone as my aunt Mary's eyes bulged down the hall. I suppose the inappropriate behavior was my way of dealing with all the changes . . . and the pain. The pain of dealing with death for the first time as well as the pain of being constantly bullied during my first year of middle school. It would be one more year before Asperger's was officially recognized as a disability within the *Diagnostic and Statistical Manual of Mental Disorders IV* (DSM-IV). And it would be at least three years before my own diagnosis at age fourteen.

I was twelve years old in the summer of 1994, when my grandmother finally died at age seventy. We were on vacation at the New Jersey shore. My father spoke for all of us when he sighed, "Thank God that's over." Hundreds of miles away, it was raining briefly until a magnificent rainbow graced the sky.

When my grandfather developed congestive heart failure five years later, he checked into the hospital for the last time. Even if someone had waved a magic wand to halt the atrophy of his heart, it would not have reversed the damage already done. The machines infusing him with artificial life were shut off as we waited.

On the eve of my grandfather's funeral, Tom slept in his sleeping bag on the floor of my room and we both had a lot of gas, either from our irregular meals or the emotional turmoil.

"Hey, Tom? Do you know what a Dutch oven is? It's when a person farts inside their bed and then traps a victim underneath the covers."

But I did not asphyxiate Tom, and chose to challenge him to a farting competition instead. (By age seventeen, I had finally learned there are appropriate times and places for inappropriate behavior.) The baritone orchestra continued for about ten minutes until a very impressed Tom said, "God! I think your last one stained the sheets." I registered this as his concession, although he would probably beg to differ. As I lay my head back on the pillow in victory, my mind began stringing together sentences capped with rhyming words.

Your big eightieth birthday party was supposed to be at my
house this weekend. Although a funeral was not what we
had in mind,
I am grateful for the time we did have together. The
seventeen years we were given to bind.
When I told you about my dreams you would never
laugh . . . you would never scoff.
You taught me many lessons. You told me that if a man
were to ever hit a woman, then that man's hand should
fall off.
You showed unconditional affection toward all your
grandchildren, never shy about dispensing advice.
When I got some of my writing published, you said
something I thought was very nice.
You said, "I had a great-grandfather named Wolfe
Saperstein, who wrote books in his Russian homeland.
"It is a very tough field to get into, but I guess any field is.
So go for it! Take a stand!"

My eulogy brought tears to the other mourners, as my other
cousin Catherine's eyes widened into saucers when she learned I
had composed most of the poem in the limousine. During the
time of my grandfather's death my Asperger's syndrome was in
remission (or at least my problems associated with the condition
were). I was earning outstanding grades in all my classes, girls
were going out with me, I had a small circle of friends, and my
behavior in Millerton was dramatically maturing. The day before
my grandfather was buried, I acted as a chauffeur for my aunt
Mary, who never drives, and finally became a role model for the
younger children. Only four years earlier, my six years younger
cousin, Patrick, was acutely aware I was less mature than him.

I am still haunted by the afternoon he blurted out: *"Oh, Jesse. You just got so weird after you had your Bar Mitzvah!"*

My parents still refused to tell family members about the Asperger's and strongly discouraged me from doing so. Sometimes parents reluctantly confide in their close relatives because they are ashamed of their child's obnoxious behavior. They desperately want everyone to understand their child's behavior is not a character flaw or a by-product of poor parenting. Maybe if my inappropriate behavior continued well into my teenage years, my mother would have sat everyone down for an intervention-like meeting. But Asperger's syndrome is often a roller coaster of extreme highs and lows. The demons finally relented, as did the need to explain my behavior.

My family revealed the AS to my aunts, uncles, and cousins when I was in my mid-twenties—once I had a string of personal and professional accomplishments under my belt. My aunt Sarah seemed almost relieved when she responded, "Well . . . we always did have an inkling." Nobody asked any questions, just like we never asked why my youngest cousin, Patrick, did not walk until he was at least two years old. Or why Tom would do just about anything for attention especially on his birthday. Like the evening he grabbed my grandfather's shofar from a shelf of heirlooms and put the sacred ram's horn to his lips like an Orthodox Miles Davis. "How about a big birthday blow!?" These acts of childish disrespect often tested my grandfather's anemic patience . . . threatening to induce his fourth heart attack.

Sometimes I walk to the Millerton Public Library, where the children's section has been dedicated to the memory of Irving and Shirley Saperstein. It is a posthumous thank-you for their lifetime of humanitarian contributions, which my family heard about for the first time at the dedication ceremony in October

2004. Nobody would have guessed they died with a small fortune, much of which was quietly given away. Families received donated clothing from Saperstein's Department Store after their houses burned down. And I'll never know how many times they wrote substantial checks to fix internal problems that were not covered by Millerton's treasury. Or how many lives were saved by the defibrillators purchased with the money they donated to the fire department. It also did not surprise me that my grandfather contributed money to support the battered women's shelter down the road. My grandparents were rarely honored for their contributions, because most people did not even know about them. In Judaism, the highest acts of charity are gifts given anonymously.

I should probably stop visiting their old house, however. It just makes me angry.

My second childhood home still exists, although it is nothing more than an un-nostalgic shell of its past enchantment. The new owners have made numerous renovations. There aren't even any pinecones left to kick because the pocket-size forest has been removed. I harbor a fantasy of sneaking inside the house, just to wander from room to room revisualizing the static beauty—the furniture and Judaic heirlooms—as they once were. Of course, this will remain a fantasy, one I will never act on. I've accumulated some modicum of good judgment throughout the past twenty-eight years. Furthermore, I know that waving my diagnosis like a white flag will not guarantee immunity within a judicial court. I will continue to entertain my childish fantasies, but I'm cognizant these choices usually come with adult consequences.

We seldom get together in the Millerton area, and the dynamics of our gatherings are radically different these days. Instead of helping Tom build a cabin of Lincoln Logs, he is helping me light my cigar with the "adults" in eyeshot. It still does not seem natural, and I'll continue looking over my shoulder in anticipation of being reprimanded. When our memories turn to Millerton, we try not to remain bitter that the magic was taken away so abruptly. In fact, we should be grateful that, with my grandfather's history of health problems, the dance lasted for as long as it did.

I also live with the regret of not telling my aunts, uncles, and cousins about my Asperger's much sooner. It would have explained my erratic behavior during the dark intervals, as well as saved my parents the stress of pretending nothing was wrong. We should have told them and trusted they would not have reacted too harshly or gingerly. They would have had the chance to see the gifts of AS that are now visible in me as an adult—when my weirdness is obscured under the gray haze of cigar smoke. The smoke eventually clears, but the Millerton Magic returns wherever the setting may be. And to my surprise, it's even more magical in adulthood.

ELIZABETH WEST

Let me embrace thee, sour adversity, for wise men say
it is the wisest course.

—WILLIAM SHAKESPEARE, *KING HENRY VI*

I can see why tourists shell out large amounts of money to swim with the dolphins or stingrays. Dolphins and stingrays are docile organisms with perpetual smiles, even though these expressions may mask contempt or distress. (I once heard that dolphins suffer from chronic ulcers when humans constantly impose themselves within their habitat.) And as stingrays caress our scuba suits like aquatic angels, we momentarily forget that Steve Irwin was sent to his watery grave by the venomous tail of a "smiling" stingray. Human beings are social animals, and frolicking with these happy-looking creatures makes us feel cared for . . . even loved. We enjoy being flattered without acknowledging the possible dangers of trusting a proverbial wolf in sheep's clothing.

Parents also lecture their children about "stranger-danger" and the kind, old lady who bestows an apple on some naive fairy princess. As a young child, I was educated about strangers by reading the Berenstain Bears and watching a live-action Winnie the Pooh special. While censoring the grisly realities of child molestation and even murder, these innocuous venues taught me that some adults do not have my best interests at heart. Even though I am no longer a defenseless child, the dangers have not subsided. I have long been susceptible to the charm of flattery without realizing the consequences. Most of the time, I am just grateful to be part of the social world. That is, until an experience opens my eyes to the dangers of being too trusting.

My life's roller coaster of severe highs and lows hit a prolonged high in eleventh grade. As a junior in high school, I was relieved to see that things were finally getting better . . . dramatically better. My learning disabilities in Math and Science improved for the first time in years. I also caved in to my mother's haranguing and joined the staff of my high school newspaper. Article after article was pounded out as I helped our staff win second place in New York State for Best High School Newspaper. I also threw my hat into a national writing contest with an entry that made it to the state level. The subsequent compliments and catered award luncheons spiked my self-esteem to an incomparable lifetime climax. For the first time, I felt liberated from the Asperger's syndrome, as though it no longer existed.

More victories followed. The super-potent medication Accutane terminated my chronic acne outbreaks forever. I also discovered the glory of blood drives and continue this bimonthly ritual with a morbid passion to this day. The bullies and insults disappeared almost completely as I fashioned age-appropriate retorts for benign teasing.

"Hey, Jesse! How small is your dick?"

"It's only two inches, dude . . . from the *ground*!"

And finally, I began going out on dates with girls—even beautiful ones—for the first time ever! Extreme social ineptitude was no longer a haunting appendage of Jesse Saperstein's sad life. And then I fell in love with the standard keyboard, as my arched fingers moved with rapid-fire precision. My ability to pound out at least fifty words a minute allowed me to further compensate for my social deficits . . . when the Internet entered my life.

It is no small wonder many Asperger's sufferers fall in love with their virtual universes and are more comfortable typing into an electronic box to a faceless individual. The Internet is the only technological medium that allows us to talk to a woman without worrying about our monotone voices destroying an already-fragile first impression. I was able to reinvent myself as the returning America Online chimes became an aphrodisiac and took away some of the factors that had previously thwarted my social progress. And just when life could not get more euphoric, I received a very sweet and flattering email from a young woman I had never heard of before. Her name was Elizabeth West.

She wrote, "My name is Liz. I have seen you around school and think you are a nice person! I was always too shy to come up to you and say 'hello,' but maybe you would like to email me back and tell me about yourself." I took her up on this offer, and we started communicating on a regular basis. Liz also introduced me to one of her female online friends, Erin Azalia, with whom I connected on a platonic level. But I had much broader expectations with Liz. The words "I am sorry, but I like you more as a friend" would have been the worst type of curse words. With Liz, I needed more and refused to settle for anything less.

Liz struck me as an unusually empathetic person who could accept and even appreciate my Asperger's quirks. When she called my house, I listened as she gushed about her ambition to someday become a special education teacher. Liz was also impressed with my involvement in a school program called the Buddies Program, which let me serve as a role model for a mentally handicapped student. She told me, "It is really nice to meet someone like you. Someone who gives something back." We had several conversations, well into the summer months, and burned up the Internet phone lines with our AOL emails. At long last . . . we made plans to meet in person for the first time.

My first date with Liz was canceled because she had to have an emergency hernia operation. We met a couple of weeks later at a local diner, and my knees promptly buckled upon seeing how beautiful she was. Elizabeth West was more than just a freakishly attractive woman. She was a concept . . . an archetype, if you will. Elizabeth West was a composite of all the women I was sometimes sensible enough not to pursue because of the inevitable heartache that comes from asking out the most genetically endowed women. Someone like Liz would have rejected me, along with 98 percent of all the other young men in a typical high school. She had long blond hair and a waist so slender I just wanted to cup both hands around it while swaying it back and forth like an erotic human Slinky. I could not recall seeing her immaculate figure in the school hallways, however. She explained that her family moved around a lot and had enrolled in a neighboring school district the last few weeks of the school year. This was only my third date of my entire life, and it felt like I was sitting with Britney Spears. (In 1999, Ms. Spears had not yet succumbed to the decadent repercussions of fame and still monopolized my fantasies.) I told Liz about some of my dreams, including my desire to write a book someday. She replied, "It is going to be so hard, but that is how it is with anything in life. If it were easy, then everybody would do it."

To my disappointment, a school acquaintance named Cara was also sitting with Liz. As my old soccer coach would say, "The girl was as homely as a hedge fence." Cara represented the antithesis of physical beauty or what would happen if David Bowie and Olive Oyl conceived a daughter during a night of hot, drunken passion. She was skinny, flat-chested, and looked like a platypus. Her complexion, courtesy of mild acne, was also tinted in a perpetual blush. Worst of all, Cara seemed to have absolutely no redeeming qualities and always went for the psychological jugular. In class, she would pepper me with questions like "Um, Jesse? I am sorry to bother you, but I am wondering if you ever masturbate?" When I sheepishly gave her an honest answer, it caused her to laugh at me even more. Like the one between the Egyptian plover and the crocodile whose teeth it cleans out, the friendship between these physically dissimilar women was possibly a symbiotic relationship. Liz enjoyed hanging out with Cara because her beauty was exaggerated in contrast to Cara's plainness. In return, Cara got to experience the thrill of popularity while being sheltered from potential taunting. Cara, however, was unusually cordial during our lunch and seemed genuinely interested in being friends. Liz and I promised to keep in touch throughout the summer as we walked each other to the parking lot.

Liz and I lost touch for a few weeks when she attended an arts camp in Maine . . . and then she promptly severed all contact with me while ignoring my constant emails to her. Plenty of young adults would have gotten the message and eventually "backed off." I, on the other hand, continued to pursue her with a relentless determination. I sent more gingerly worded emails and spent hours loitering online hoping she would sign on. I called up Cara to find out why her friend was ignoring my emails.

Cara just sighed and mumbled, "You know, maybe this should tell you something." Then she related stories about Liz's manipulative personality and suggested I would be better off forgetting about her. I still craved Liz with a physical and emotional hunger that intensified each time she did not answer my emails. By this time, she had mutated into a human narcotic with the power to destroy me through abrupt withdrawal.

Liz finally replied to my messages, and there was indeed something wrong. I was relieved to learn that I had done nothing to offend her and she was not trying to terminate our friendship. But the story she told sent chills down my spine and would no doubt have a profound effect on any potential relationship. Liz had been raped and was now pregnant.

While at the Maine arts camp, Liz and a few of her platonic male friends went camping in the woods. They had toted along some alcoholic beverages, and she trusted the guy who handed her the beer spiked with a date-rape drug. Liz was repeatedly violated by at least one of her "friends" before her naked body was discarded in the woods like a slimy plastic bag. She was left alone, unconscious, and exposed all night long. When Liz finally squinted against the July sunshine . . . the memory literally throbbed inside her.

Liz wrote emails confiding about how scared she was. She said, "I don't know what is going to happen to me. There are a lot of choices I am going to have to make very soon, but I'm not prepared to make them." She also told me about how ashamed she was and understood if I never wanted to talk to her again. But her ordeal began to draw us closer, as I wanted to help in any way possible. At one point, I was contemplating offering her money.

I further admired Liz's character when she took drastic steps to seize back her life. Liz chose to abort the fetus as opposed to accepting premature motherhood or the anguish of adoption. She was attending weekly church services with Cara and was in the early stages of filing sexual assault charges against her assailants. Liz also invited me to her school's homecoming dance.

A few days before the dance, I learned a traumatic lesson about the dark side of computers. Online predators are not restricted to pedophiles and amoral scam artists. About six months into our friendship, I finally discovered that Liz and her circle of friends were not real.

When I say, "Liz was not real," I mean the whole thing had been a hoax perpetrated by a group of mean-spirited students at my high school and at least one individual from a neighboring school district. My virtual tormentors were fully cognizant of my severe naiveté, which they decided to milk as long as possible.

When I confronted them online, they referred to me as "the biggest fucking loser ever" and told me it was my own fault for being "stupid enough to believe them for six whole months." The following day I refused to go to school and lacked the energy to do anything beyond lying in bed for hours, thinking about killing myself or someone else. I had no choice other than to accept that I had been a victim of what we now refer to as "cyberbullying." But in the waning days of the last millennium, no official term existed.

Despite the cruelty of the extended hoax, I will acknowledge a small trace of redemption. My online tormentors made strong efforts to stop the prank . . . on countless occasions. They tried blatantly ignoring me for weeks in hopes I would finally forget. When this did not work, they tried creating an elaborate lie. They even concocted tales about Liz's malicious personality in hopes of diffusing the fictitious relationship. When this tactic also faltered, they became frustrated as well as intrigued by my blind persistence. Finally, they decided to string me along until I eventually gave up or the prank died a natural death on both ends. But I would never have stopped, and had every intention of taking my pursuit of Elizabeth West to the utmost extreme. Around the time the prank finally stopped, I was formulating plans to roam the hallways of Liz's alleged school.

Like many Asperger's sufferers, I have become familiar with the condition's darkness. Obsessive persistence can be credited for most of my life accomplishments and a handful of neurotypical friendships. On occasion, it has served as an invaluable asset. More often than not, however, my persistence has festered into an Achilles' heel with serious consequences. The metaphorical horse continues to sustain postmortem bruises long after most people would have been sensible enough to walk away.

Nursing an intense grudge for years can lead to poor physical health and chronic emotional distress. One of the common expressions regarding forgiveness is "Holding a grudge is like eating rat poison and waiting for the rat to die." While I agree with this cliché, forgiveness is a personal choice. A person does not have to forgive in order to successfully move on with his or her life. Telling another individual to let something go is supposed to serve as firm but well-meaning advice. This advice, in reality, is harsh as well as grossly ineffective. For someone with Asperger's syndrome, it may produce the opposite effect by encouraging the person to hold on to the grudge even more tenaciously. It is also not fair to give someone advice most of us cannot follow ourselves. If we take a meditative breath to conjure the Aspergishness within our hearts . . . within our souls . . . we can come up with more creative solutions.

The grisly retaliation fantasies eventually dissipated as I

found an appropriate way to fight back . . . using the same tactics. I took on the anonymous persona of a fake screen name and IMed one of the male participants under the ruse of being an attractive female *very* interested in getting to know him. I encouraged him to brag about his little prank, pretended to be impressed, and subsequently printed out the entire IM conversation. I then turned over his inadvertent confession as well as countless other past emails to my high school administration, who could not give my tormentors more than a stern lecture and call up their parents, considering the victimization occurred outside of school. Cyberbullying was perfectly legal when I was a teenager and still is ten years later. Once in a while, a cyberbullying case will just barely make it into a court of law. In order for this to come to fruition, however, a little girl from Dardenne Prairie, Missouri, had to hang herself in a closet and an adult woman had to be involved in the hoax. I sadly did not witness my victimizers crying and shaking in their boots . . . but I had acquired some amount of closure.

Before "Elizabeth West" forced herself into my life, my naiveté and vulnerability were crippling. For example, I used to pretend to be like one of the big shots in gangster movies by carrying excessive amounts of cash for no reason. It also never made sense to lock my bulging wallet in my gym locker (at least until one of my classmates relieved me of at least $100 one afternoon). Asperger's robbed me of common sense, while my accidents were always waiting to happen. My mother even said, "I think it is a good thing this horrible thing happened to you this year instead of later on in your life." Liz West made an unsuccessful cameo appearance in the tale of the chiropractor who nearly coaxed me into signing a yearlong treatment plan for appointments I did not need to correct a nonexistent life-threatening spinal defect.

Her essence returned in the salesman who failed to sell me a pyramid scheme. It is also critical for parents and adult role models to remind a child that the senseless and malicious actions of a few people do not necessarily represent the opinions of the majority. By the end of high school, a lot more people had given me credit for what I had achieved. With every new triumph, Liz West and her circle of friends faded further into obscurity. They were nothing.

Just a painful life experience.

The majority of bullying is perpetrated by cowards who are convinced their victims do not have the physical or mental faculties to fight back. Cyberbullying is arguably the most cowardly form of childhood bullying because the tormentor is operating from the safety of his or her own home . . . cowering behind an anonymous screen name . . . saying things he or she would never have the courage to say to the victim's face . . . imposing themselves into someone else's haven. It disgusts me how we live in a society that takes a lackadaisical stance toward such malice.

As is customary with all my ex-tormentors, I wonder how they are doing. Have they found happiness, sought redemption, and overcompensated for their former acts of evil? It is possible they are just as mean-spirited now and adhere to the adage "You cannot make chicken salad out of chicken shit." I also wonder if they have brought children into the world. Are any of them as atypical as myself?

I feel guilty fantasizing about such poetic justice, but I always wonder whether any of my ex-bullies will raise children affected by Asperger's syndrome, or another mild disability carrying severe social repercussions. Will they see shadows of their past victims and worry as the school bus departs? Perhaps the one light in this grim scenario is imagining that these former tormentors have transformed into vigilant parents. They will work harder to preserve their child's self-esteem while preparing that child for the often unfair realities of being unique. And "Liz West" has since evolved into an androgynous term I use to describe the evil that sometimes seeps under the door like noxious mist. It will never be capable of empathy or mercy, and can only register Asperger's syndrome as a weakness to be exploited.

COLLEGIATE CHALLENGES

My reasons for attending a small, liberal arts college in Upstate New York had little to do with academia.

I applied for Early Decision to terminate the college application process by December 1999 and force Mrs. Stewart out of my life. My parents had hired a college advisor they treated like a reincarnated Hindu deity because of her access to the Gates of Higher Academia. I merely thought she was a relentless bitch for canceling my family's annual vacation to Ocean City, Maryland, in favor of "college touring." She terminated what was supposed to be a blissful week of Maryland blue hard-shelled crabs, ocean swimming, and the mini–roller coaster that sends its passengers clanking up a dark, vertical tube before free-falling into the briny, summer night. But something else truly "wrapped up" my decision to commit to Hobart and William Smith Colleges in Geneva, New York.

When the backwards-walking tour guide mentioned the Egyptian mummy, I demanded she take us to see it. The tour guide admitted, "Wow! I think you are the first person who has ever asked to see the mummy." Gasps and apprehensive chuckles tittered among the rest of the group while we walked down the stairs.

The library's basement resembled a tiny museum straight out of a low-budget Indiana Jones epic. Display cases contained salvaged relics from ancient battleships along with other archaeological treasures. The mummy was something out of a sinister Grimm's fairy tale—a gruesome Snow White who perished from waiting in vain for Prince Charming's kiss. The plaque indicated it had once been a woman in her mid-twenties, who died of unknown causes. Its face reminded me of a wizened, petrified apple, and everything below was wrapped in jaundice-colored bandages. This actually seemed like an ideal way to ride out eternity if I someday became very wealthy. I'll bequeath every cent to a college campus with one morbid condition. In exchange for my vast fortune, the campus would be legally bound to display my mummified remains in one of the main buildings . . . forever. A plaque about my life's accomplishments shall be nailed above the glass sarcophagus along with photographs taken in the prime of my life. This arrangement would allow me to remain the center of attention and inspire students—despite the radical handicap of being *dead*.

The first two weeks of college felt like a cushy summer camp with reasonable traces of academia. My hands began flapping in ecstasy upon learning that my earliest class took place at 1:55 p.m., which was a welcome extreme to being forced out of bed before 7:30 a.m. for thirteen years. My parents could no longer dictate how I spent my free time, as I pilfered hours watching TV past one o'clock in the morning. I became fond of *TV Funhouse*— an X-rated composite of *Howdy Doody* and *Pee-wee's Playhouse*. In a cartoon parody of *Dennis the Menace*, "Mischievous Mitchell" terrorized his Jewish neighbors by shooting ham cubes into Mr. Goldstein's mouth with a slingshot and constructing effigies of Hitler. In my darkest hours, I even watched reruns of *Gilligan's Island*, while wondering what compelled them to take along so much miscellaneous shit for what was supposed to be a three-hour tour. I also fell in love with the laid-back, sophomoric ambience of a freshman dormitory, which is almost as necessary as the academic climate. There is something magical about walking into a dorm room and being greeted by obscene posters. Most college dorm rooms are decorated with posters giving sentient characteristics to bowel movements and featuring satirical anti-masturbation public service announcements. I became obsessed with the masturbation poster where a newborn kitten is being pursued by two Domo-kun (block-shaped Japanese monsters) through a lush field of poppies. A caption states, "Every Time You Masturbate . . . God Kills a Kitten. Please Think of the Kittens," followed by the anguished face of a wide-eyed kitten. The most cherished novelty of college, however, was shedding the negative reputation that had haunted me throughout my formal education. And I still managed to squander a Golden Opportunity after finally shutting off the TV.

My high school reputation was promptly reconstructed with bricks of nonconformity. As long as my actions were not illegal, I felt justified imposing my eccentricities upon the student body. But this sense of entitlement came prepackaged with draconian consequences.

Time management is a weakness for many on the autistic spectrum. Like a seasoned Olympic athlete, I was sprinting around campus to just barely make it to appointments on time. The constant running led to doomed first impressions as cries of, "Run, Forrest! Run!" echoed at least two times a day. I also arrived on campus with an arsenal of bouncy balls merrily launched against campus buildings. Other mistakes were unavoidable only because they seemed like a good idea at the time.

In high school, some of my classroom humor was appreciated and/or tolerated in moderation. Therefore, I resumed the role of class harlequin in a course called Youth Culture, when the professor discussed sexual harassment by women in positions of power. Considering my only experience with reverse sexual harassment was from the 1994 film *Disclosure*, I entered the discussion with a long-standing bias. Although the Michael Douglas protagonist *did* suffer personal and professional repercussions, most of mankind would still concur that there are far worse crimes against humanity than being forcibly seduced by Demi Moore. Without raising my hand, I blurted out, "Oh, God! Are you kidding me!? There *should be* more women who sexually harass men! I would actually enjoy that kind of victimization!"

As I waited for the laughter, a female student turned around and sniped, "Would you feel the same way if your girlfriend were with you? *Or your mother!?*" Everyone else nodded in collective disgust as I sunk into my chair . . . frustrated and embarrassed.

I also assumed that the same romantic tactics used in high school would surely generate success in the college world. My obsession with attending senior prom had driven me to ask out any attractive classmate with an XX chromosome. I had every intention to persist with this plan until all feminine resources were exhausted or I was forced to pay airfare to a Las Vegas escort service. After enduring two dozen rejections or vague responses, one of the high school beauty queens actually consented. She stood out like a genetically enhanced orchid against a bed of dandelions—blond, blue-eyed, and somehow willing to overlook my social deficiencies. A few months later, my hand still tingled from the sensory imprint of purple silk on a swirling dance floor. My conquests at college had a different outcome, however.

All freshmen were handed a Hobart and William Smith directory containing the contact information of everybody on campus. This literature was appropriately nicknamed "The Stalker Book" and quickly became my bible. As if I were a cold-calling stockbroker, my Friday and Saturday nights were depleted phoning random acquaintances to ask them out on dates. My romantic standards were relatively straightforward. I mean, she needed to have at least one ovary, a pulse, and ideally be unsaddled with a boyfriend back home. One dozen phone calls is all it took before I ascended to the status of a campus pariah and was forced to take responsibility for my behavior.

When I was an adolescent, my father always admitted, "I really worry about you, Jesse. You have the freedom to be as weird as you want. But you are going to face consequences." I had long filed this away under the category of "bullshit"—until it was too late. Toward the end of my sophomore year at college, my best friend, Karl, was kind enough to give me a voyeuristic vantage point on the situation. He shared the roster of creative monikers spawned from my erratic behavior: Sketchy Jesse, Scary Jesse, the Psychopath, the Stalker, Running Jesse, the Wanderer. (The Wanderer may have alluded to my habit of aimlessly trolling the streets after two o'clock in the morning.) Ignorance about

Asperger's syndrome was what had created the mess, although my unapologetic flamboyance had the effect of dousing a raging tire fire with gasoline.

My contact with female acquaintances was also initiated by delivering birthday cards containing three pages of nonsensical ramblings. And if she were God-forbid-not-home, that supposedly gave me the right to plant my ass next to her door like a demented groupie until the young woman hopefully returned by midnight. One of my birthday targets later admitted, "What you did on my birthday really creeped me out. Nobody sends long cards to people they hardly know. You talked about weird things in your card, too. I did not need to hear about how our 'final exams will engulf us like a demon until we expunge them from our souls!'"

I replied, "Exactly! That was the whole point! And if you don't like strangers sending three-page birthday cards, you should have told me before I did it."

The bizarre birthday cards would continue for eight years, with continuous modifications and compromises. I still send birthday cards to obscure acquaintances, but always disclose my mild autism in a handwritten disclaimer:

I have something called Asperger's syndrome and this is how I choose to communicate with people. If you do not wish to receive future cards, please give me the courtesy of telling me this yourself.

I majored in English despite nursing lifelong fantasies of becoming a medical doctor. The chance to relieve suffering and terminate diseases could turn into the perfect varnish to my social deficits. However, despite having incredible professors, my performance in college Biology made a compelling argument against this notion throughout my senior year.

In Organisms and Populations class, I was nearly reduced to tears while waiting for freshwater zebra mussels to filter a petri dish of algae. Cells and Molecules class did not fare much better, as we bred fruit flies in a genetics experiment. Having used a flat hose to siphon gas into their test tubes, I dumped these anesthetized bodies onto a microscope slide prior to examining their reproductive organs. Seizing a once-in-a-lifetime opportunity to use the expression in a literal sense, I cried out, "Oh, God! They're dropping like flies!" and earned a few chuckles. After determining the ratio of males to females, I struggled to come up with a hypothesis based on eye color among the second generation of fruit flies. A student muttered, "Thirty-two thousand dollars a year and I'm staring at damn fly crotches all afternoon!" I silently echoed his disgruntlement. African frogs met a more grisly fate as we crushed their frozen testicles into a petri dish of unfertilized eggs. Our professor explained, "These frogs have generously *donated* their scrotums for our benefit. African frogs also served as the first home pregnancy tests because the females would start to ovulate in the presence of a pregnant woman's urine." The two consecutive C-pluses in senior Biology were a stark contrast to how I'd started out. My freshman year had concluded with one A-plus, one A, five A-minuses, and one B-plus. My academic performance suffered for the first time, although my social realities on campus had finally improved. And for the first time in my life, I discovered that I was not alone.

Campus served as a haven for other misfits who were learning disabled or were just downright odd. Hobart College was also my first time meeting other individuals with Asperger's syndrome. Like me, they had experienced an unusually turbulent start.

Mark was diagnosed shortly before arriving on campus, and his AS was compounded with attention deficit/hyperactivity disorder. Mark always had to be "doing something," and this manic energy made it difficult for him to maintain friendships. I understood it would be *hypokriticol* (note another spelling I like to use) to attack him for his verbal diarrhea, although he seriously overstepped his bounds one afternoon after contacting me via AOL instant message. Mark wanted to know if I planned on attending the Yom Kippur celebration at the Jewish Culture House. I typed, "Sure Mark! I'm coming."

"How r u cumming?" he replied.

"Huh?" I wrote back.

"R U cumming in a tissue or all over the keyboard?"

I did not know him well enough to understand his humor and chose to terminate the conversation. One minute later, the phone rang, and it was Mark calling to apologize.

Mark's drinking was responsible for a dismal grade point average, which nearly got him expelled, along with honing his computer skills to start a fake ID business. While this may have ingratiated Mark among his beer-guzzling neurotypical peers, it did not exactly aid the precariousness of his situation. Fortunately, the solicitous deans got Mark into counseling and his academics steadily improved. Then there was Henry.

Henry arrived on campus with a wardrobe of ostentatious suits. It could have been seventy-five degrees outside and poor Henry looked like he was en route to the funeral of a Russian dignitary. One of the suits even had a thick cape. Along with his naturally pallid complexion, the suits really did make him look like something out of a contemporary Bram Stoker film. Henry kept to himself, which was a stark contrast to my tactics of aggressively imposing my friendship and asking out half the girls.

Like a dog that had been kicked one too many times, he some-times recoiled when sympathetic students tried to initiate a con-versation. Any trust he'd once had was probably beaten out of him a long time ago by high school tormentors who devoted their energy toward making his life miserable. At some point in college, he must have hit rock bottom and was no longer able to handle the unrelenting isolation. The peculiar suits steadily evolved into buttoned-down white shirts . . .

The three of us began our collegiate experience battling our respective demons—exacerbating what is already a difficult tran-sition for most students. But all it took was some minor person-ality tweaks to pierce the shield of isolation. One day, I made the conscious decision to quit running and became more judicious about how many William Smith women I asked out on dates. These compromises melted some of the harsh judgments and even earned some stray compliments: "You've really changed, Jesse. You are not as aggressive with women these days."

But I was desperate to be liked by all the students, which proved to be no more realistic than changing the Upstate New York climate.

My social trials were hardly atypical for autistic college stu-dents thrashing in a quagmire of neurotypical peers. Some stu-dents may retreat into a state of mental hell when the anguish yields little mercy. They also become vulnerable to bitter iso-lation, academic failure, dropping out, or even suicide in the most extreme cases. If I had attended another institution, one of these options could have seemed like a sensible alternative. But at Hobart, I had "the chance" to succeed and gain a bit of self-understanding in the process.

My eventual success on campus never came from "letting things go" or accepting some of life's realities. Being judged as honest and reliable infused me with a sense of empowerment that compensated for what did not always come from my peers. My professors viewed me as unusually conscientious and were magnanimous enough to tolerate my benign abnormalities. When two sympathetic professors offered me extensions on assignments, I walked through the city of Geneva to track down their residences—melding the damn paper with their door using half a roll of Scotch tape. Like Martin Luther pounding his *Ninety-five Theses* onto the mahogany door of All Saints Church . . . I stepped back a few feet to admire its radiance. My college years taught me that social acceptance could only be earned through compromise, but I still had to be myself once in a while. My efforts to placate the rest of the campus by pretending to be "normal" resulted in pleasing virtually nobody while making me just as miserable and angry as I'd been for much of my life. It was important to sometimes act "weird," but I would seize opportunities to justify my "weirdness" through acts of benevolence. Hobart and William Smith Colleges gave me that chance often enough. There were also romantic victories, tolerance, second first impressions, and even awards. I just had to fight a little harder.

PSYCHOBABBLE

Dr. Finch tried repeatedly to engage my brother in therapy,
all to no avail. My brother would sit politely in the doctor's
inner office, his gigantic arms slung over the back of the sofa,
and he would grunt, "Huh. I still don't understand why I need
to be here. I'm not the one who's eating sand."

—AUGUSTEN BURROUGHS, *RUNNING WITH SCISSORS*

Apparently, the common vibrator served as a medical device to treat hysterical women during the coke-snorting reign of Dr. Sigmund Freud. *Hysteria* was once classified as a physical and mental illness affecting only women. (Even its Greek root, *hustera*, means "womb.") The psychological stigma of hysteria as a female problem did not change until soldiers began returning from the Great Wars with profound mental distress. Anyway, when an afflicted female patient was wheeled into a hospital's psychiatric ward, the doctor would insert the reverberating phallus into her vulva. It always seemed to have a wonderful calming effect. Imagine that!

I have never actually believed in psychotherapy and am convinced the majority of professionals need a couple dozen sessions themselves. The foundations of the science of psychology must be taken with a grain of salt because not every single word is gospel. Some of them are downright erroneous. For example, Dr. Freud's theories are based on a small group of female patients . . . several of whom he engaged in sexual relations. It is not entirely uncommon for a patient to bond with his or her psychoanalyst—in fact, it is considered part of the treatment—as the boundaries become quite blurred. But this is just fucking ridiculous! In some cases, particularly with Dr. Bruno Bettelheim, psychology has served as a tool to enhance the doctor's ego while spreading mass ignorance. And even fear . . .

If I had been a little more cognizant as a seven-year-old, maybe I could have sensed the fear in my parents' eyes. Until Asperger's syndrome was officially recognized as a U.S. disability in 1994, my lack of empathy was attributed to a personality defect, something that had to be corrected as soon as possible. Like so many parents desperate to reach their enigmatic children, mine assumed professional intervention was the best solution.

When I was six, my parents sent me to a benevolent psychologist who won me over with comic strips during my first session. Calvin from the *Calvin and Hobbes* comic strip was routinely threatened by some dim-witted bully named Moe (the proverbial Coke machine with a head) and often escaped the beating by outsmarting his nemesis. But Moe, when he occasionally worked through Calvin's mental games, would promptly beat the living shit out of Calvin. The last frame of the strip always showed Calvin lying in a mangled heap of limbs as wispy, animated lines of pain lingered overhead.

Calvin always seemed to be burdened by multiple, unrelenting strikes. He was unusually short, goofy looking, with porcupine-like hair, and seemed to have no friends, with the exception of that stuffed tiger he toted around like a security blanket. Even in the magical world of Comic Strip Land, we can ascertain that Hobbes the tiger is just a tool Calvin uses to cope with his sad realities. Charlie Brown, for that matter, is another comic strip hero prone to constant failure, frustration, and abuse from his peers. If this were not bad enough, it seems the perpetually bald Charlie Brown was cursed with childhood alopecia. If Calvin and Charlie Brown ever broke free from their animated shackles, they would be ideal candidates for the psychiatrist's couch. And their futures would most likely be grim and hopeless.

Calvin's parents would grow concerned over his obsessive fixation on what everyone else registers as an inanimate stuffed tiger. Calvin's maturity seems to be perpetually arrested, and he has yet to exile Hobbes in some dusty crawl space, as his peers did with their stuffed animals years ago. "It's time to let go of Hobbes, already!" his parents would shriek. "You are thirteen years old and still carrying around a stuffed animal like a little baby. The hours you spend with this stupid thing, you could be making real friends!" They would grow even more apprehensive when Calvin revealed that Hobbes has been giving him advice . . . ordering him to commit acts of petty vandalism. They would shell out $200 per session just to be told their son *does not* have childhood schizophrenia.

Shortly after his fourteenth birthday, Calvin's folks would sneak into his bedroom to throw Hobbes in the garbage minutes before the sanitation workers arrive. And this desperate act of tough love would backfire when Calvin ended up in the children's psych ward after coming after his parents with a steak knife. He would now be an unemployed, Zoloft-medicated thirty-year-old who is doomed to live in his parents' basement forever . . . collecting action figurines and marinating in bitterness. Hobbes robbed him of invaluable time that should have been spent developing friendships with other boys and romantic relationships with girls. His parents robbed him of Hobbes—the closest thing he would ever have to a best friend.

Charlie Brown's future would probably be grimmer as he nurses a misogynistic hatred toward little girls (often portrayed by the late Charles Schulz as manipulative, bossy, and even cruel). After growing tired of being teased by Lucy, he would take her football and throw it at her face . . . breaking her nose explosively as she screams through a gushing stream of blood and tears. This act of rage would earn him a three-day time-out in juvenile hall before Lucy's parents dropped the charges. He would grow tired of constantly failing, all the while waiting for the breaks that always came to his peers, but never to him.

The day would come when Charlie Brown finally stopped fighting, as his self-esteem plummeted to a suicidal level. As a last resort, his parents would send their morbidly unhappy child to a therapist who would psychoanalyze Charlie Brown with that trademark incoherent warbling associated with adult dialogue in the *Peanuts* cartoons. In the meantime, Linus would be handed over to the same therapist because of his delusional and compulsive belief in the Great Pumpkin. The *Peanuts* gang would disband, as childhood friends usually do in adolescence, although Charlie Brown finds new companions. He would be embraced by a group of neo-Nazi skinheads as his high school years faded away in a haze of marijuana and aimless hatred. Aside from the occasional odd job, forty-year-old Charlie Brown would be chronically unemployed and spend five nights a week cowering in the same bar, reminiscing about those glory days, which never really existed in the first place.

I visited the psychologist almost every Tuesday for five years, and the anemic office plants are etched in my memory. These visits were extremely necessary during transitional periods, when the dark side of Asperger's erupted with a vengeance. At the start of third grade, my teacher would often send me home with notes delineating my bizarre, inappropriate behavior.

Dear Mr. and Mrs. Saperstein:

I had to discipline Jesse this morning. A little girl just received news that her mother gave birth to a healthy baby boy. Jesse blurted out in front of the class, "I hope he came out retarded."

Sincerely,
Mrs. Smith

When my father asked me, "Do you even know what 're-tarded' means?" I shook my head. Yes, it is true I was ignorant of its literal definition of "having an IQ below seventy." But I knew it referred to something very negative . . . something to provoke a hostile reaction from my teacher and classmates. I probably said what I said out of jealousy, to purloin some of the attention and happiness another child was receiving. My behavior changed the day Mrs. Smith finally decided she had had enough.

"Jesse," she snapped. "Push your desk to the front of the room and put it in front of mine!"

For the rest of third grade, my desk was adjacent to Mrs. Smith's. The change of scenery inspired a radical change in be-havior as I settled into a comfortable niche as teacher's pet and a schoolboy crush formed.

Despite being young and attractive, poor Mrs. Smith was af-flicted with chronic arthritis.

"Here, Jesse. Could you open this for me, please?"

She would often slide across a can of Pepsi, thawing with beads of condensation, which I would pry open with agile eight-year-old fingers. It was a euphoric feeling to earn the respect of an authority figure and have an important role within the class. Throughout the rest of third grade, my behavior improved as the negative behavior began to diminish. And yet . . . the psychologist remained part of my life, while robbing me of time that should have been devoted to video games, syndicated TV shows, and other pleasures of an American childhood.

The presence of the good doctor was justified once again when I left this comfortable niche for another brutal transition. At the start of fourth grade I was confronted with challenges such as bullying and the peer isolation that would probably plague me for the rest of my life. My methods of dealing with the pain could have been construed as harbingers for an antisocial adulthood. Some afternoons I would punch myself in the face as classmates looked on in horror. Once in a while I would also slide my hands down my pants to touch myself with a sheepish grin plastered on my face.

"Jesse . . . what are you doing?" Unlike some other Asperger's adults, I was able to get this behavior out of my system long before it became an act of public indecency, subject to arrest.

The one "climax" of my therapy took place inside the waiting room, with the good doctor absent. I was nine years old when my father and I arrived at the office a few minutes early. I headed to the magazine rack in search of a *Highlights* magazine—the children's version of *Reader's Digest*. But I was getting too mature for these babyish publications, and another magazine piqued my interest. It stood out from the others like a sexy oasis within a sterile desert. An issue of *Vanity Fair* featured a very pregnant (and naked) Demi Moore in her infamous 1991 photo shoot. She was covered under pounds of body paint . . . glistening like an erotic rainbow. With that in mind, the shrink may have been inadvertently responsible for a welcomed neurosis that manifested thirteen years subsequent to our weekly sessions. That is, my obsession with *Desperate Housewives* and an affair with a forty-year-old English teacher . . .

"You cannot make an omelet without breaking a few eggs."

Practical advice may cause the AS patient to do the *wrong* thing. A compromise must be drafted and agreed on by both parties. And furthermore, the solution to a problem may be achieved with nonsense, silliness, inappropriate behavior, and weirdness. My own psychological chemistry is that of a sponge absorbing multiple forms of negative energy. Over the years, I have developed more constructive management techniques to replace punching myself in the face or touching myself in public.

The shrink always talked about an evil force that he called "negative energy." Negative energy was supposedly associated with obsessions, anger, grudges, and flapping my hands in front of my gimlet-eyed cats while spouting gibberish. As a six-year-old, I automatically assumed negative energy was the unscientific term for an actual viscous fluid flowing through the circulatory canals like poisonous endorphins. I pressed for a more specific description and wanted to know what happened if too much negative energy built up at once. He shrugged his shoulders and answered, "You're more tired than usual and get things like headaches or stomachaches."

That did not sound so bad and was not an incentive to radically alter my personality. After all, the biology of someone with Asperger's syndrome *is* partially comprised of negative energy!

AS individuals are incapable of completely letting go of ideas, obsessions, anger, bitterness, silliness, and more. This vestigial mental clutter cannot always be purged from the subconscious, although it can be controlled.

It is too myopic, however, to claim that the therapist failed. Asperger's syndrome would not be recognized by the DSM-IV until one year after my parents finally ended these therapy sessions.

I always say, "The only true negative energy is anything that negates positive action."

Most professionals fail to understand that only one type of negative energy is genuinely negative. Real negative energy occurs when someone neglects to use anger as a catalyst for positive accomplishments. Negative energy was never the boogeyman that the psychologist always claimed it was. In fact, it has been responsible for countless accomplishments. Among other things, it was the reusable fossil fuel propelling me on foot for 2,174 miles on the Appalachian Trail, from the state of Georgia all the way to Maine.

While I am still convinced many therapists could qualify for analysis themselves, perhaps this is not always a negative. In fact, maybe this is the way it should be. Think of how many people would benefit from being treated by a counterpart . . . a successful, adult role model also flush with composite weirdness.

When my young Asperger's patients entered my office, I would understand that it is not fair or ethical to dispense advice I cannot follow myself. Therefore, my words of wisdom would be fiercely unorthodox, but effective.

ME: How do they make fun of you in school? I'll bet they ask you things like, "Hey, Steve? Sorry to bother you, but do you ever masturbate?"

STEVE (nodding shamefully): Yes. All the time!

ME: I am not surprised. When I was your age, the other kids asked me that until the cows came home! But let me tell you two things you need to know. First of all, every single man does it. It is as common as shaving or brushing our teeth. When I first discovered it as a preteenager, it felt like someone had built an entire amusement park in my room or at least installed my favorite arcade game. Second of all, your classmates are most likely demolishing an entire box of tissues as we speak! The reason they are making fun of you is because they are ashamed of themselves.

The patient's eyes would widen into saucers upon hearing an adult speak so crudely.

Then he would smile and collapse into hysterical giggles. We would exchange respective war stories while reminding each other it is all right to be "weird." I, Dr. Jesse Andrew Saperstein, would trample the professionally mandated eggshells of the doctor/patient relationship by attending my young patients' school performances to honor their bravery. When the young gentleman became obsessed with girls, I would help him find a healthy balance between "backing off" and "stalking." Together, we would map out a plan of action for both the romantic pursuits and the inevitable rejections.

And of course, my patients would double over in violent chuckles when I told them stories. I would explain how the founding father of psychotherapy used cocaine and had sex with his female patients. And the true origin of the vibrator . . .

ALL THE WORLD'S AN AWKWARD STAGE

Laser pointers and cigarette lighters are flickering on and
off like fireflies. The crowd is like a giant organism. It feels
good to be standing above it, separate, with a little elbow
room and a fence to keep people at bay.

—JOHN ELDER ROBISON, *LOOK ME IN THE EYE*

As a preteenager, I would do just about anything for attention.
Many of my stunts involved bizarre, inappropriate behavior
intended to get a reaction from my "audience." Plenty of outrageous antics occurred in my synagogue because I knew the
Sunday school teacher would never call home. Like the morning
I shut my eyes and challenged myself to pace around the entire
fourth-grade classroom—without bumping into anything. I could
pick up the teacher yelling at me as the students murmured with
an all too familiar tone of disgust. A pile of books was knocked
over as I felt the Talmud's spine land sharply on my foot. One
time I rattled the cage of the principal by giving the class a brief
rendition of "Jingle Bells." Or I responded to someone's accusa-
tion of me "being gay" by following a male student around the
class, trying to sit with him. My behavior in the synagogue was

also an attempt to rebel against a religion I did not always condone or understand. It is still difficult for me to warm up to an
institution that forbids the consumption of lobster and Maryland crabs, my two favorite delicacies.

Other inept class clown routines followed throughout most
of my childhood. One of my most cherished memories took place
during an eighth-grade gym class while my teacher was taking
attendance. My fiber-enriched breakfast started to haunt me as I
sensed the unrelenting buildup of gas within my colon. If I had
hung in there for a few minutes, the pressure would have re-
treated to my intestines or I at least could have found an appropriate time in which to relieve myself. But what is the point of
remaining uncomfortable? More important, why squander a
golden opportunity to incite a mini-riot?

Without a moment's hesitation, I deftly planted my butt
cheeks on the glossy floor and let out flatulence that reverberated
through the entire gymnasium. The following scene was reminis-
cent of the parting of the Red Sea in Cecil B. DeMille's epic *The
Ten Commandments*.

Kids scurried away from my ass and cried out in unison,
"EEEWWWWW!" I put my head down and donned an expression of mortification. Beneath the feigned embarrassment, I was
pleased with myself while fantasizing about when I would have
this combination of audience and acoustics again.

My inappropriate behavior was a constant throughout most
of my childhood, as was the negative attention from teachers and
peers. Provoking the negative attention was far more satisfying
than being ignored. If friendships were beyond my reach, I would
haphazardly grasp for a substitute.

As we all know, trouble and ridicule are usually less elusive
than positive attention deriving from hard work and accomplish-

ments. My inappropriate behavior peaked around age fourteen when I decided to "pull a boner" in ninth-grade Math class. Literally . . .

The lesson was on quadratic equations, although I chose to direct my visual energy elsewhere.

I burned an optical hole through my gorgeous, twenty-three-year-old teacher as she delivered the lecture with a scratched overhead projector. My auditory cavities were stimulated by her velvety voice, along with other physiological regions. Her hands moved with unusual grace as she wrote the mathematical figures with a dry-erase marker. In the process of pining for her, I failed to notice my very prominent erection. Unfortunately for me, everybody else in the class . . . did.

The classroom transformed into a symphony of pointing and giggling. "Look! He is pitching a tent" and "Ohhh . . . shit! Jesse's got a boner!" The story would also be registered in the indestructible file cabinet marked "Weirdness and Public Humiliation of Jesse Andrew Saperstein." My peers always found joy in rummaging through the archives to remind me of such incidents. (They could never focus on all the days when I did not have a boner in Math class!)

The pointing and audible whispers continued. Even my luscious Math teacher took a fleeting glance at the source of the commotion as I basked in the attention. The stubborn bulge refused to dissipate, however. Perhaps the mini-riot would have died down a lot sooner if I had adjusted my pants and leaned forward in my seat. But I was enjoying the attention. It was a psychological narcotic that satisfied millions of starved synapses. I stopped taking notes and chose to recline in my chair as a means of flaunting the bulge in all its glorious prominence.

The groans and insults were happily absorbed like spilled

Manischewitz on a Passover tablecloth. After all, any attention felt better than being ignored. It is also not uncommon for a child with AS to impose himself as the obnoxious, unfunny class clown even though his inappropriate behavior usually incites more bullying and contempt.

"Nobody likes you. You have no friends. You are the biggest fucking loser ever! Are you gay? Do you masturbate? Why are you so weird? Why do you talk slow? Why do you talk funny? God, what is wrong with you!? Maybe if you stopped being such a geek, people would like you better. Do you actually think a girl like that would ever go out with someone like you?"

Consequently, the bullying and isolation continued until I finally discovered healthier ways to gain attention.

My eleventh-grade U.S. History teacher, Mr. Walters, resembled a diminutive owl, and his mannerisms seemed to scream for disrespect. And he always said the same thing before *every . . . single* test! "Put your notes away. Books away. Cheat sheets away. No, you cannot have cheat sheets in my class during a test." Despite his excruciating dorkiness, there was something about Mr. Walters that caused us to back off and give him a break. He was the man who would become an unlikely hero for me, as well as the first teacher who taught me a valuable lesson: Once in a while, there are appropriate times for class clowning.

Mr. Walters had assigned the class an extra-credit assignment shortly before Bill Clinton's impeachment in December 1998. We had to draw satirical political cartoons to be displayed within the classroom. Due to my gross lack of artistic talent, I was the only student who opted to stay out of the project. Mr. Walters walked over to my desk.

"Hey, Jesse. Why don't you read your poem to the class? I'll count that as extra credit."

A few weeks earlier, I had sheepishly told Mr. Walters about a poem entitled "The Night Before Impeachment," modeled after "The Night Before Christmas." In my poem, Bill Clinton got into a gory duel with Lorena Bobbitt—the infamous knife-wielding, penis-amputating femme fatale who is a vestigial nineties icon. After Mr. Walters made sure nobody would be offended, I began to recite my opus.

Some of my peers could barely raise their heads from their desks as they choked from spasms of laughter.

> *I have had enough of your excuses, President Clinton. No*
> *   more ifs, ands, or buts;*
> *Because I just so happen to be crazy. And in a matter of*
> *   minutes . . . you'll be just nuts!*

The class switched from laugher to thunderous applause as Mr. Walters said, "Thank you, Jesse. We all needed that." I needed it as well. Performing showed I could earn positive attention in the most unlikely of places. People would register more than the Asperger's syndrome and would take the radical step of giving me a chance. I discovered, at long last, that tolerance and positive attention were worth fighting for.

I soon became obsessed with the stage and clawed for opportunities like a starving street mime. A couple of performances would be harbingers for more ridicule because I was either unprepared or tried to forge talent that nature had withheld (most of the time, it was a combination of both). But after each successful performance, peers who had previously ignored me began to congratulate me in the hallways. Other victories followed throughout the year. School plays, senior follies, and a fashion show in which I was a runway model were added to my growing résumé. For the first time in my life, autism did not have a negative impact on me.

I am hardly the only individual with Asperger's syndrome who has ascended to the stage to earn social acceptance and recognition. In his memoir *Look Me in the Eye*, John Elder Robison describes the contributions he made to the band KISS. As the special effects and electrical engineer, Robison designed hollowed guitars that launched sparks, flames, and pulsating smoke. His obsessive, meticulous nature also proved to be a valuable commodity. We are indeed an obscure species herded by symptoms, classified in countless clinical books and Wikipedia-ish Internet sites. Nonetheless, everybody with Asperger's syndrome is different.

John Elder Robison may be more content making a contribution from behind the scenes. As for me, all of my stage performances produced an extreme amount of anxiety before, during . . . and immediately after the performance (if there were minor flaws to perseverate over). But I craved this new type of positive attention, and performing was my only chance.

My audience fills out the room like a forest of lukewarm algae swaying to the lunar tides. Or maybe it is better described as a giant marionette suddenly animated by the Elixir of Life! A poem or skit is an unrestrained force that can effectively manipulate hundreds of people at once. These performances replenish much of what Asperger's has taken away. Successful performances paved the way for dates with beautiful girls, new first impressions, swelled self-esteem, and social recognition. The stage took away my awkwardness and made me believe I could become whatever I wanted.

As an adult, it is easier for me to talk to an audience of a hundred strangers than just one acquaintance on the phone.

Maybe it's because of the many failed one-on-one conversations I've experienced. Or perhaps it's because I crave the attention so badly. But ultimately, it's just one of the many beautiful contradictions associated with Asperger's syndrome.

On the stage, I can usually influence a positive outcome. But the performances of day-to-day social interaction can be neither rehearsed nor controlled. Every encounter requires a distinct dialogue with a unique set of expectations, and what is appropriate in one scenario may be grossly inappropriate in another. To give just one example, I honorably resigned as a salesman for Saperstein's Department Store when I learned my employment would cause my family's business to hemorrhage money.

"Excuse me, ma'am? I could not help noticing your son's name is Damien. Isn't that also the name of the Antichrist?"

She gives me a dirty look and snaps, "For your information, Damien is the name of a saint!"

Our educational system has a legal and moral responsibility to accommodate children with unique learning styles. But as teachers, parents, and advocates, we have responsibilities that extend beyond the legal requirements. It is even more critical to nurture a child's self-esteem when *the performance* falls upon deaf ears. And it will from time to time. But when the performance is successful . . . the applause will be deafening.

TEENS LIVING A GREATER CHALLENGE

I have arguments with my family like any other twenty-something adult still living at home. We yell, scream, and occasionally pound our fists on the kitchen table. Our fights typically revolve around money, my stubborn refusal to attend graduate school, and my job choices, among other common subjects. But a handful of arguments revolve around bizarre, esoteric topics. This is not the heated drama of sitcoms, because no family (fictional or otherwise) could ever conceive of such conflicts.

Sometimes we argue about the etymology of the phrase "That *really* hit the spot"—an expression I have angrily banned from the Saperstein household. I'm convinced it refers to a female orgasm and "the spot" alludes to the woman's erogenous zone. When my father says it in a breathless whisper, after a filling meal, it gives me the damn heebie-jeebies. We also argued on

Election Day 2004, after returning from a local elementary school to exercise our civic duty. As soon as the curtain closed, I rather audibly relieved myself of all intestinal pressure and was immediately reproached by my disgusted father, who understandably kept his distance . . . pretending not to know me.

"What the hell is wrong with you?" he hissed. "That curtain is not soundproof!"

I put my hands to my mouth and asked, "Oh, my God! Did you actually hear me?"

He expelled a loud sigh. "Jesse! I *actually* heard you from the other side of the gymnasium!"

I had forgotten that out of sight is not synonymous with out of earshot.

One of our most vicious arguments revolved around platelets. *Platelets!* Father made the same shuddering sound I heard thirteen years ago when my collection of snake skin landed on his leg.

"Oh, God, Jesse! Nobody does this unless they are doing it for a relative who is dying in the hospital. Nobody! So just knock it off already!"

We were fighting over my decision to voluntarily hook myself up to a phlebotomy machine twice a week (every week) to donate a bag of platelets. Donating platelets probably does not qualify as an obsession, because it is not something I *have* to do. Rather, it's a passion that blossomed over the course of a decade for me. The sensation of a mechanical beast draining a pint of my vital bodily fluids is morbidly relaxing and self-gratifying to me. I am part of a 1 to 2 percent minority responsible for saving lives. Again and again and again.

I relish everything about the process, while ogling the computer screen with childlike fascination. Blood circulates in the plastic chambers like oil in a combustible engine, as an internal centrifuge separates its components. My lifesaving bodily fluids are extracted, and the whole blood is returned in a succession of mesmerizing cold flashes. Eventually, the digital hourglass indicates the donation is complete, and the final product looks like a swollen bag of Tang. The donation begets yet another ritual when I make a trip to the nearby mall for some aimless, solitary wandering. My family will never understand why I always return for more deliberate pain, but it all stems from an original paradox: "In order to make life easier . . . it is imperative to make everything as unnecessary and complicated as possible."

When surrounded by medical equipment, I feel surprisingly at ease—which is a nice change of pace for someone who's usually invisible to other people (or, worse, avoided like a plague). The phlebotomists treat me like one of their best friends and ceremoniously presented me with a stuffed platelet doll—a hybrid of a lone flame and SpongeBob SquarePants. Maybe they secretly think I'm creepy, although this is not necessarily a negative. There is something about me that prompts them to take another look, because "normal" people would not do this to themselves for six hours a month. I also learned a long time ago that when an individual is afflicted with a social disability, the doomed first impressions can be systematically dismantled through acts of kindness or leadership.

My father and I clash over our dissimilar attitudes about life. He believes in avoiding unnecessary commitments or situations that make him uncomfortable. I, on the other hand, swear by my masochistic philosophy: "All things unnecessary are too often necessary." For me, any long-term idleness has often been a catalyst for inappropriate behavior spawned by the Asperger's syndrome . . . repelling elusive romantic partners while attracting trouble. But mild autism does come with a few redeeming qualities—specifically a compulsion to always do what I say I am going to do. From a very early age, I understood that such redemptive behavior could stimulate social acceptance. Environments that would normally react with contempt or fear would embrace me with acceptance. And even love, once in a while.

Another summer of disturbing familial conversation came to an end as I signed up to serve as a residential advisor during my senior year of college. I immediately regretted my decision when the residential education department gave me an unusual assignment: the AIDS Awareness House.

I reluctantly accepted the position while secretly worrying that I would become associated with the "gay stigma." I feared that my involvement might cause rumors to spread like wildfire when the campus came to knee-jerk assumptions about my sexuality. Ironically, despite my fears, the AIDS Awareness House brought something amazing into my life.

My duties included planning at least one major house activity. So I contacted a twenty-four-year-old man named Joey DiPaolo, who was the first child after Ryan White to go public about his HIV/AIDS. Wrongly, I had always looked at people with HIV with contempt, as though they were repeated drunk drivers with a blood alcohol level of 1.6. But Joey deviated from the usual stigma. He was a patient at the wrong hospital on the wrong day and received the wrong blood transfusion after surgery to correct a congenital heart defect.

Joey's life intrigued me because he had straddled the extremes of being condemned as a pariah and lauded as an international celebrity. More than one hundred families tried to prevent him from attending junior high school, but they failed thanks to his persistence. The firestorm launched him into the spotlight with a fan base that included Montel Williams and President Bill Clinton. After I picked him and his mother up from the Syracuse train station, one-quarter of the car ride was spent with Joey regaling me with tales about seeing the spider monkeys in Hugh Hefner's private zoo while soaking up attention from the bunnies at the Playboy Mansion's grotto. His life was a fountain of surreal stories. After an evening meal held in Joey and his mother's honor, we made our way to the conference room to set up the audiovisual equipment. I looked at the attendees and was ashamed for having not trusted the Hobart and William Smith campus to have an open mind. The Geneva Conference Room was packed with at least one hundred students and faculty members! The presentation started off with a medical lecture. Joey's mom explained the symptoms of full-blown AIDS. She also explained how a person always dies indirectly from AIDS and instead succumbs to the opportunistic infections invading the body's compromised immune system. Joey spent the rest of the presentation answering difficult questions.

"Are you ever able to have children?" one young lady asked.

"Yes, I can have children someday," Joey proudly answered. "There is a procedure I can undergo in which the sperm can be cleaned and the woman will not contract AIDS."

The most profound advice he gave us was: "If you do not have AIDS, then stay that way. If you ever do get AIDS in the future, then just take it one day at a time. And don't be afraid. Be a friend."

The speech ended with words from our college president:

When Paul Revere raced down the streets of Boston crying out, "The British are coming! The British are coming!" there was another man on the other side of town doing exactly the same thing. His name was William Dawes. People did not wake up to listen to Dawes, however. They listened to Paul Revere. Sometimes it all depends on the speaker. I think all of us have witnessed another Paul Revere tonight.

Feverish rounds of applause were addressed toward Joey and then me for bringing him to campus.

> The best way to find yourself is to lose yourself
> in the service of others.
>
> —MOHANDAS "MAHATMA" GANDHI

Partly out of codependent desperation to keep Joey DiPaolo in my life, I offered to volunteer at his summer camp for teenagers with HIV/AIDS, called Camp Teens Living a Challenge (TLC). This was hardly the first time I'd stepped on the untamed grass of a campground. As a child, summer camp often seemed like an extension of the school year where I was confronted by the same bullies and loneliness. Sometimes I did a great job of exacerbating my social isolation by collecting Japanese beetles in my Fisher-Price tackle box and thrusting the squirming mass in front of screaming little girls. When not collecting beetles, I stimmed in solitude while peeling dead bark from twigs. Toward the end of my day camp career I had finally matured and attempted to initiate friendships among my peers. But it was too late because

I had devoted about eight years to etching my Legacy of Weirdness into brimstone .

Now, for some reason, I had returned to camp offering my services as an adult authority figure.

Contrary to what you might expect, I have always despised children. They never detect a disability—only weaknesses to be exploited. Children are manipulative, selfish monsters with an innate desire to prey on the gullibility of those with Asperger's syndrome. They always seem to judge me as an adult version of the peers they love to torment. Now I had intentionally thrust myself into the lion's den.

The iPod-sporting, hoodie-wearing teenagers stumbled off the charter bus onto the YMCA campground, feigning arrogance and toughness. Despite their best attempts to look street smart, they looked like they were about to enter the Enchanted Forest, where malevolent creatures dwelled within. They were in for a life-changing experience, and so was I. My perspective was about to be radically altered forever.

Prior to Camp TLC, I assumed the only vulnerable HIV population was composed of reckless individuals who didn't care enough to take commonsense precautions. It is true what they say about the word "assume," because it really does make an "ass" out of "u" and "me." But mostly *me*. Every camper had contracted HIV via prenatal transmission and faced personal challenges that dwarfed any obstacle I'd either faced or surmounted in my lifetime.

As an adolescent, I viewed my life as a tapestry of nuisances—Hebrew school, Sunday school, abusive peers, apathetic teachers, acne, impromptu erections, loneliness, severe sensitivity to the sound of nail biting and foods containing artificial cheese. Even character-building rites of passage, such as braces and my Bar

Mitzvah studies, were part of a conspiracy to create unnecessary misery for me. But, as I would soon discover, my grievances paled in comparison to the hurdles these kids faced.

The campers had to take medications with brutal side effects—vomiting, diarrhea, bed-wetting, and cramps. The side effects were exacerbated by new medications or prolonged lapses in their regimens. It was a relentless (and possibly lifelong) catch-22. The most enforced policy at Camp TLC was for all campers to take their medications. No dose was ever neglected. Bargaining was also forbidden.

A child does not see the logic of taking caustic medications when he or she is superficially healthy. Even responsible adults would balk at taking vile-tasting cough syrup every day. A young person with AIDS may neglect to take his or her medications and live in pristine health for years as the HIV virus hoards its energy. They are feeling much better but are in actuality getting sicker by the day. Eventually, the HIV virus mutates into full-blown AIDS; the compromised immune system rolls out the red carpet for opportunistic infections and possibly even death. They live in fear of their dormant illness as well as the rest of their community reacting with violence if they ever found out they have the disease. Education should have exterminated such groundless fear among the public two decades ago, but it hasn't. Camp TLC, however, restores something life takes away.

Outside Camp TLC, the term "AIDS patient" does not literally refer to an individual receiving treatment in a hospital setting. "AIDS patient" is a slur just like a racial epithet or any other vicious insult. It points to the degenerate, the lowlife, the untouchable waiting to die in some grimy corner. Therefore, it was no surprise the campers had co-opted the slur, turning it into a term of endearment. "AIDS patient" was tossed around all week long, followed by plenty of giggling and smiles.

In many ways, Camp TLC seemed like any other summer camp. There were pranks, arts and crafts, a lake for swimming, and lots of the usual urban legends that circulate all summer long. A fictional chemical, for example, called neon peon taints the lake water and reacts to human urine by dying the campers' shorts pink.

But Camp TLC was too special to be called a normal camp. Most of the time, it straddled the line between a fantastical high school sex ed class and a spa for children, complete with high-priced Manhattan masseuses donating their services. The childhood cruelty I remember from summer camp was nonexistent even among the most vulnerable.

I did not have that much hope for Jason when our paths first crossed, and I knew he was doomed to experience a week of ridicule or being "politely ignored" because nobody knew how to approach him. First of all, Jason was white, which made him a minority in a population of societal minorities. A severe speech impediment exacerbated by cerebral palsy took away his ability to communicate without the use of American Sign Language (ASL). I did not anticipate the moment Jason started tearing up the dance floor with Justina and Yvette—two of the most achingly beautiful campers in the entire group. Nobody could have anticipated the moments of bonding among a population whose dissimilarities should have been a melting pot for chaos. The sick, healthy, physically and mentally handicapped, and the downright weird of different races and religions all merged together within Camp TLC.

In the sexual health seminar, I stifled a giggle as one of the campers tested the durability of a condom by stretching it over his head—like an elastic bathing cap! An instructor rolled another prophylactic over a green phallus that looked more like a cactus than a dildo.

She held up a red condom. "Some of the flavored condoms contain sugar that kills the natural bacteria inside the vagina. But this is a sugarless, strawberry-flavored condom. Go ahead and taste it if you want!" Not understanding what she meant by "taste it," I popped the latex sphere in my mouth as a little girl clasped her hands on her freckled cheeks like a female version of Macaulay Culkin on the *Home Alone* poster. "Oh, my God! she groaned. "He put the entire thing in his mouth!" As with a stick of fresh bubble gum, I experienced a sharp burst of flavor and blew a phallic bubble. In a moment of panic, I yanked the condom out of my mouth. What if I propelled it to the back of my mouth and reflexively swallowed it? What if it caused me to choke, lose consciousness, and force the hospital to surgically remove it from my throat? The doctors would probably save my life, although the oxygen deprivation would result in a lifelong vegetative state. They would keep me alive at the taxpayers' expense so I could inadvertently serve as a morale booster. My tragedy would lift the spirits of new paraplegics or patients recently diagnosed with terminal pancreatic cancer. These tragic souls, forced to come to terms with their grim realities, would react with either heaving sobs or catatonia. The nurses would have a ritual of wheeling melancholy patients past my room and pointing. "You think *you* have it bad! Wait until you hear about what happened to that poor bastard!"

They would abandon all sense of decorum and forget that a soul once occupied this barely living shell—someone with dreams.

They would laugh until tears rolled down their cheeks ... drowning out my respirator's hum. Their mirth would intertwine with an excruciating truth—that life (or at least its essence) could potentially be extinguished forever by accidentally choking on a flavored condom! For a short while, they would forget they may never walk again or had only four months left to live.

The constant physical activity combined with the camp food sent my intestines into overdrive. The campers and staff members eventually got used to my constant flatulence while accepting it as a harmless personality quirk. One night, I feel asleep on one of the couches and was later told the campers had gathered around me to time "farts" like Boy Scouts measuring the distance of a storm through intermittent thunderclaps. In the mornings, my ass usurped the standard rooster call as fellow staff members wondered aloud, "What the hell? Is there a war going on? It sounds like kamikaze pilots!"

One Asperger's trait I've always considered an asset is my obsession with being on time. It's a haunting lesson I learned in school, when teachers would harass me for being thirty seconds late. Once I learned punctuality, it became a constant for me. To my dismay, the campers at Camp TLC were always running late, staying in bed until the last possible minute and ignoring all our attempts to extract them from their scratchy blankets. These minor conflicts prompted me to employ a common Asperger's strategy: thinking outside the box.

When Kevin refused to get out of bed for the third time, I brought out the heavy artillery. I warned him, "I've had enough! If you do not get out of bed in ten seconds I am going to stick my ass in your face and fart! Drastic times calls for drastic measures!"

"Oh, no, son!" another camper replied as Kevin finally started to get out of bed. "That is *way* too drastic. That's like using weapons of mass destruction in a game of UNO!"

The campers did not prove to be the malevolent reincarnations of my childhood tormentors I'd feared they would be. It also was not necessary to educate them about Asperger's syndrome, because they did not mock me for my intrinsic weirdness. They judged me on my efforts to help them enjoy their week, as I speared a hundred worm entrails on campers' fishing lines. Furthermore, I stopped distinguishing them as hosts to one of the deadliest diseases from the last century. After all, this was the magic of Camp TLC! It quelled the din of ignorance and prejudice that echoed in the real world. It also functioned like a sanctuary, where the unfair realities of the world had a divine obligation to "just back off."

The long-term effect the campers had on me was an emotional buoyancy that propelled me through overwhelming odds. Seven months after camp ended, I would start walking the Appalachian Trail from Georgia to Maine, intent on completing the entire journey. The hike would also garner statewide media exposure while raising an exorbitant amount of funding for Camp TLC. I was introduced to an extreme most Asperger's individuals will never experience in a lifetime—massive positive attention from complete strangers blind toward the mild autism. I would hike while holding on to Camp TLC's magic and feeding off the campers' energy. Their spirits sustained me like a can of Red Bull—an internal explosion created a new reality I'd never imagined was possible. Camp TLC also reminded me once more that there would be future venues where I would anticipate hatred or ignorance, but would be embraced with acceptance. Sometimes even love.

When the campers' applause finally died down after I announced my plan, it occurred to me the Appalachian Trail is more than 2,100 miles long and stretches from Georgia to Maine. It takes an average person at least six months to complete, and is arguably the most challenging footpath in the world. And I had absolutely no hiking experience whatsoever! This time, perhaps I should have kept things simple and continued impaling myself with a needle for two and a half hours per week.

SUMMITING THE STIGMA

What we call the beginning is often the end. And to make an end
is to make a beginning. The end is where we start from.

—T. S. ELIOT, "LITTLE GIDDING"

It is fair to say that when I committed to hiking the entire Appalachian Trail, from Georgia to Maine, to raise funds and awareness for Joey DiPaolo's camp for young people with HIV/AIDS, I could not have imagined the challenges that awaited me—physically, emotionally, and even socially. It was an adventure in every sense of the word.

The biggest challenge—tougher than endless hours in the wilderness, extreme weather, unfamiliar insects, and the unbelievable scourge of chafing (a much bigger concern than it sounds)—was the exposure to other people, each one there for his or her own reasons and carrying his or her own baggage. I went through five long-term hiking partnerships on the AT, each one more eccentric than the last. But their flaws were easily forgiven based on what they brought to my hike.

There was a fiercely neurotic forty-eight-year-old man who was unpredictable, to say the least. Sometimes he would throw a minor tantrum if I walked too close behind him or suggested he take an Advil to alleviate his muscle pain. Other times, he was lackadaisical about infractions that would be distressing for most individuals. For example, when I accidentally peed into his Gatorade bottle, I braced for a strangling that never came.

After that partnership dissolved, I found myself hiking with a squabbling married couple whom I nicknamed Skillet and Bottle. Sadly, they would succumb to divorce shortly after terminating their hikes. Both were twenty-one years old and often wanted me to mediate their conflicts. Like marijuana, wine, medication, sexual pleasure, and other factors that have both benefited and perverted mankind, the Appalachian Trail has a sinister side some people discover the hard way. The Trail has destroyed its share of once-stable friendships, romantic relationships, and even marriages.

One thousand miles into the journey, my life took on the fantastical tone of a *Desperate Housewives* episode when I ended up hiking with two attractive young grandmothers. The first of this matriarchal succession was a forty-four-year-old woman I called Skylarke.

Skylarke's adult life had commenced at age fifteen when she gave birth to her first child, Jeremiah. She loved her thirty-year-old son very much, while supporting him as he battled against two societal strikes. He was gay and he was legally blind in both eyes. But like most parents, Skylarke just wanted her child to be happy and experience profound vindication for his suffering.

It was pleasurable spending time with Skylarke. In fact, I felt comfortable confiding in her about my Asperger's syndrome as she elaborated on Jeremiah's challenges. Too many people, as

Skylarke explained, were reluctant to take the "radical step" of giving her son *a chance*.

Skylarke was aware Jeremiah would have to fight harder to be acknowledged as well as earn the achievements many able-bodied individuals take for granted. And I sometimes think of the anguish my own parents had to endure. As my mother once said, "There is no feeling worse for a parent than knowing your child is in pain." Like Skylarke, they wondered if I would ever find stability or a semblance of happiness.

Skylarke abandoned the Appalachian Trail fourteen hundred miles into the journey. As it turned out, she could not have anticipated what was waiting at the end of her long, green tunnel. A few months later, she sent me a long email—updating me on her post-AT life. Her son and his partner had gotten married, and the wedding, near their home in Spain, was a joyful and beautiful celebration.

> *Hope is the glimmer of light in a parent's*
> *darkest hours.*
>
> —Janis Saperstein

The second young grandmother was a woman I called Sleeveless, who had recently experienced the birth of her first grandchild. Sleeveless was the ultimate superwoman of the Appalachian Trail, and I was rather happily delegated to the role of her sycophantic sidekick. She bossed me around constantly, in a benevolent manner that suited us both. I was also captivated by her surprising strength. Every year brings a handful of hikers tormented by Biblical Bad Luck who probably should quit, but don't. Amid bouts of severe chaffing, giardiasis (a mild form of dysentery), Lyme disease, foot rot, financial troubles, and more ailments . . . they slog onward. Sleeveless caught her share of hardship, including being attacked by a raccoon (she boldly pried the beast's jaws open with her bare hands).

Hiking with these fearless grandmothers taught me a wealth of information—though not enough to begin to fill the vacuous abyss of everything I could not, did not, and *never* would understand about women. Trying to win an argument with a woman is about as effective as using a wineglass to bail out the *Titanic*. In contrast, simple phrases like "That is a great idea," or "You are absolutely right," can really make a difference. Women also have hypersonic senses, like the visually impaired comic book hero Daredevil. Just as Beethoven could detect piano vibrations to compose his opuses, Skylarke sensed my impending flatulence from the other end of a long log or would become enraged by the faint clicking of my cell phone keys on the other side of camp.

Each new hiking partnership brought something incredible to the table and was dissolved amicably when the union ran its course. And just like a codependent serial dater . . . I immediately found another companion after the previous one had left. Most of my hiking partners were physically stronger than I and pushed me through periods of lethargy with tough love. Furthermore, these friendships were never artificially sustained by guile and remained symbiotic in nature.

My final batch of hiking partners—Holden, Gettysburg, Nessie, and SBD—was more age appropriate, and for the first time in more than two thousand miles, the Appalachian Trail's terrain no longer resembled the polygraph profile of a pathological liar. After all that mountainous terrain, we had finally entered the One Hundred Mile Wilderness. Aside from a few goose bumps, the terrain rarely rises above twelve hundred feet and yields consummate, orgasmic flatness! Like many other hurdles throughout the journey, its malevolence has been greatly exaggerated, and by then I was no longer intimidated by menacing statistics of failure.

My new, age-appropriate hiking partners and I squandered a pristine, early October day playing beer Frisbee, which is essentially an athletic version of college beer pong. The objective is to knock over a Nalgene bottle fifty feet away and force one's opponent to consume a cup of flat Budweiser. I personally considered it a ridiculous waste of the day, especially because the culmination of our 2,174-mile journey was no more than a week ahead. It was like a team of frostbitten climbers pausing thirty minutes before the summit of Mount Everest . . . to play hacky sack for ten hours! Nobody ever wins beer Frisbee, because the plastic disk always ends up trapped inside a towering sequoia tree or nobody wants to touch it after an intoxicated player shoves it up his rectum. But I wanted to "fit in," so I agreed to this plan as long as we night-hiked the first thirteen miles of the One Hundred Mile Wilderness.

Colder weather cleared out many of our miseries, including Maine's infamous black flies. Leaves began to fall from the trees, stirring memories of foliage-filled autumns of childhood. (For me, fall will always be about Halloween, the infantile pleasures of which I chased long after it stopped being cute or appropriate. I continued trick-or-treating well into adulthood, as neighbors began making comments like "My! Aren't we big!" instead of cooing over my Halloween costume.)

Despite the beauty around us, SBD stumbled down the terrain like an angry dog on tranquilizers. Everybody gets a trail name that is often a tweak on their physical appearance or a quirky personality trait. For instance, I received my trail name

LoJack when the other hikers discovered that my mother had forced me to hike with a GPS locator device. SBD's trail name was an acronym—Silent But Deadly—because of his tendency to emit an odor of unclassifiable foulness, like the rancid juice of a skunk. So foul that one had to scrounge for hyperbolic adjectives to properly describe it. Some hikers have a system of yelling, "Courtesy," when they are about to pass gas, so those walking behind them have a fighting chance to move out of the way. SBD never took the "radical step" of giving us a warning, however. But these colorful flaws had absolutely nothing to do with why I passed judgment on him.

SBD was not the lovably inept buffoon often portrayed by Steve Carell and Will Ferrell. These fictional failures are the ones I have always sympathized with and even admired. They try *so hard*, but fail constantly as a consequence of being unable to accept their innate, natural ineptitude. But SBD was the archetype of the young man who self-destructs once the curtain closes on his high school glory days. His athletic talent did not translate into the professional leagues or even a partial college scholarship once the limelight fizzled upon graduation. Since then, he had carved out a transient existence while bouncing from one mediocre job to the next. Yard work . . . busboy . . . janitor. SBD reminded me of those sociable booze hounds who populate bars like corporate shills while scanning the crowd for the homecoming queens of yore. SBD even had a criminal record for infractions like public urination and DUI. The last DUI offense had resulted in a jail term of nearly an entire year, although SBD did not seem to show any remorse. He spoke of his punishment as a draconian consequence for a victimless offense.

Throughout my adult life I have always prided myself on giving people a chance before condemning them. But perhaps all of us are walking hypocri*** or are, at the very least, vulnerable to not practicing what we preach. We may even do it unconsciously. For instance, I sometimes question the fanatical tree huggers who populated my liberal arts college. How many of them have sheepishly ducked out of an organized nature walk to personally hose down the base of an oak tree? This is arguably the worst defilement one can commit against any living thing or monument. Are they even aware of their own hypocri**? But it was painfully easy to judge SBD as a lowlife regardless of whether or not I knew him well.

My contempt toward SBD was placed on a back burner as new conversational topics saturated the night along with our misty breath. Holden mentioned that another hiker had been describing some of my strange habits, including a night spent loudly clapping my hands in an attempt to smother the sound of someone else's snoring. "The guy was terrified of you," Holden told me. "He thought you were going to murder everyone in the shelter that night!"

I cringed as I remembered the night in question. To my surprise and relief, SBD came to my defense. "LoJack, that guy is ignorant." I told them about my AS, and they accepted it without judgment or much surprise. I suddenly wanted to burst into tears of relief, and I no longer condemned SBD for his past transgressions. As a matter of fact, I desperately wanted to hug him. Maybe the true natural magic of our journey was the way it allowed us to give each other more of a chance . . . to chisel off the initial plaque and *just take another look.*

My fellow hikers and I actually reeked of failure. Their lives had been scarred by divorce, alcoholism, limited ambition, romantic rejection, broken homes, learning disabilities, dysfunction, job terminations, imprisonment, social isolation, bitterness, and other unfair realities. Like Al Bundy from *Married with Children*, they were a magnet for failure whether they deserved it or not. And yet . . . they were able to complete a task that 90 percent of individuals who start are doomed to fail. So many of these alleged "losers" find redemption on the Trail as they continue walking to escape their demons.

Seven months earlier I had had my own assumptions about the 10 to 15 percent of hikers who were destined to complete this 2,174-mile death march. I assumed they were brawny overachievers, and the Appalachian Trail would become another notch in their lifetime of accomplishments. But the majority of survivors are similar to SBD and even me. We are stereotypical *losers* who are succeeding with an almost impossible task.

My family's silver Odyssey van was the antithesis to the wilderness I had immersed myself in for the past seven months as it barreled toward Mount Katahdin at 5:15 a.m. It took less than forty-five minutes to devour the distance it takes two full days to cover on foot. A vehicle is the ultimate mileage monster as well as a constant temptation to "skip" miles when the concept of an Appalachian Trail thru-hike is to complete every single mile. To do otherwise is considered unethical by the hard-core hiking community. I heard the distinct pinging of gravel pellets against the muffler, and it still surprised me how acute my senses are when faced with modern amenities. I had only four steep miles left to climb, but they seemed more like a chore than ever. All I could think about was returning to the synthetic never-never land of comfort—where a magical stream of clean water comes from a tap. A three-day stay in this decadent hotel had duped my body into believing the hike was finished as my right leg seized into a protesting cramp.

It is easy to understand why so many people choose to terminate their Appalachian Trail hikes before taking the "radical step" of giving it a chance. Most of us are used to surviving a week of school and/or work while buffering the tedium with caffeinated beverages, restaurants, the Internet, television, etc. From the very first day of my hike, it was as though four hands smashed through the bowels of hell to strip away these layers of comfort. Nothing was left except a raw tangle of nerves, which screamed in agony with the slightest touch. But just as quickly as the Appalachian Trail strips away these layers of comfort and familiarity, it also offers an incentive to build them back up through any means necessary.

I engineered a sense of comfort by singing the *Mickey Mouse Club* theme song as well as countless other Disney songs. In fact, over the course of the hike, I dramatically augmented my obsession with the Disney empire. Walt Disney won the most Oscars of anybody; Disney and Ernest Hemingway served in the same infantry during World War I; Mickey Mouse was created on a train; my father once saw Walt Disney at a world's fair; and *Snow White* was the first full-length animated feature. My mind was once cluttered with a twelve-hour night-shift job, credit card bills, romantic rejection, personal hygiene rituals, social anxiety, college compositions, and familial conflicts. These layers have also been stripped away, as my uncluttered imagination is allowed to run rampant with nonsensical thoughts, fantasies, *and games*! Sometimes, for amusement, I composed vulgar poetry with a Southern belle's accent:

Ahh, farhted once.

Ahhh, farhted twice.

Ahhh . . . farhted Chicken Soup with Rahce!

And to combat the frustration of faux summits, I deliberately replaced my panting with sounds of a burgeoning orgasm. "Ohhhh . . . baby! So good. Oh, jeez Louise!"

The first two miles of Mount Katahdin are surprisingly tame, especially when compared to all eight relentless miles of the Approach Trail of Springer Mountain. Its terrain boasts consummate flatness while being occasionally crisscrossed by streams migrating away from their original source. My parents struggled to keep up because they had the foolish intention of trying to climb the final peak with me. If this were any other mountain, I probably would have been considerate enough to slow down. But I did not seem to be going that fast.

I overheard my father saying, "Let him go off on his own! I do not want to hold him back."

Mount Katahdin's terrain unfolded like the ominous "clanks" of a roller coaster, and the vegetation thinned after two miles had lapsed. Trees turned into arrested saplings with their roots in perpetual distress. The vegetation towering over me minutes earlier began to shrink, while I half-expected a camouflaged army of Lilliputians to start launching arrows the size of sewing needles. Pretty soon, all plant life was replaced by alabaster boulders the size of small cars. The more cumbersome boulders had handrails drilled for the hiker's convenience, as I climbed above tree line for the first time since New Hampshire's White Mountains. And for the final time, I straddled the craggy backbone of a mythological beast with an occasional shock of burrowed, ancient fur.

My father has lectured me on countless occasions, "People do not appreciate it when you impose yourself on their lives, Jesse!" But on the afternoon of Tuesday, October 11, 2005 . . . all tact became null and void upon my reaching the summit of Mount Katahdin.

I took a few moments to admire the billowy, cumulous clouds hugging its jagged peaks before running my fingers over the plaque's crenulated letters. Believe me, social graces were the last thing on my mind as a disposable camera was shoved toward weary day hikers who had no choice but to participate in my command photo shoot. A sardonic doppelganger of Kathy Griffin finally snapped, "What do you want now? Oh! You want me to hold the banner?! Fine!" The fiery redhead and I unfolded the banner signed by every Camp TLC camper. We braced the mammoth ribbon against the wind, which seemed to assault us from all directions. Some man handed me a can of Budweiser lined with condensation and said, "Here! You've been walking for seven months and deserve this more than I do."

I accepted it without any hesitation.

It would be naive to assume that this mythic hike allowed me to *let go* of my rage, which will forever remain an appendage of my Asperger's. The rage comes from years of failing and watching my less socially challenged peers succeed with relative ease. I am also quasi-prepared for the consequences of imposing myself on people who choose to condemn AS as a character flaw in need of correction rather than compassion. And they certainly do have a point. To someone dealing with a more serious disability, the mildest form of autism would probably seem like winning the genetic lottery. Compared to the extreme impairment of mental retardation or advanced Alzheimer's (the latter of which my grandfather struggled with), what I have to contend with is not so tenacious. My escalating drive to impose myself upon the world will probably come with consequences as people also criticize me for siphoning support from more severe disabilities.

I'll never stop fighting and will eventually accept that cynicism will be my constant foe. And unfair criticism will be cynicism's offspring. In laymen's terms, no human being is immune to cynicism and criticism even when buffered by profound heroism. Christopher Reeve was attacked for his Super Bowl commercial where his head was digitally superimposed on a mobile actor of similar girth and height. His "creepy" commercial supposedly gave false hope to people who would never walk. John F. Kennedy was criticized after challenging the American people to send a man to the moon by the end of the 1960s. Too lofty and unrealistic a goal, his critics claimed. And I wonder whether my mentor, Joey DiPaolo, ever had to endure criticism for his "crime" of contradicting the HIV/AIDS stigma. How many people had already made up their minds to condemn AIDS as a self-inflicted illness caused by reckless decisions? How many of his critics wanted Joey to just sit down? For these reasons, Joey remains my hero, along with the late Randy Pausch, author of *The Last Lecture*. Their heroism comes from surpassing such obstacles to play the brutal hand they were dealt.

The poison from the past was in remission. The scars, however, will never completely recede because some pain is too intense for the body and mind to ever forget. My negative energy had been catalyzed and refueled into a mission more profound than anything I could have anticipated. And even though my seven-month climb had officially ended, I fully intended to hold on to its lessons.

This hike was the first time I no longer had to fight to belong and was quickly embraced by a community. Some amount of stock was invested in first impressions, although they were absolved in a baptism of collective perspiration and goodwill. The Asperger's syndrome allowed me to succeed where so many others (with or without a disability) have failed. Therefore, I felt vindicated by the fact that every mile was hiked with Obsession, Perseveration, Anger, and Weirdness—aspects of my personality that were once perceived as demons, not assets. Instead of sabotaging my progress, they were employed as tools to conquer what is arguably the most treacherous footpath in the world.

Later that night, I paced around the Mount Katahdin Inn instead of going to sleep at a reasonable hour—in an attempt to preserve the freshness of the thrill of victory, and also to relish the feeling of relief: For the first time in seven months, I could return home without dwelling on failure. But my strolling became aimless and restless as I received an ugly preview of the days following my homecoming. Months earlier, a former AT hiker had warned, "You are going to feel just like the Energizer Bunny trying to force your way through a brick wall."

Mixed in with my sense of accomplishment was a fear of what lay ahead. I was worried about leaving a world where everything made sense. The Appalachian Trail had proven to be the Great Equalizer, a strange and special place where fewer people called me names like "Sketchy Jesse," "The Psychopath," weird, creepy, or loser. It was easy to be successful on the Appalachian Trail compared to the reality awaiting me back home. On the Trail, we had admired one another's persistence and were usually magnanimous enough to not always judge by first impressions (eventually). Success on the AT was gauged at the pace of two and a half miles per hour; the statewide media attention quenched my hunger for positive attention; and I worked to raise awareness for young people living with HIV/AIDS.

Joey and the young adults at Camp TLC taught me that you have to love yourself enough to try to convince others to do the same. Now I was prepared to push on to the next stage . . . often armed with a dim headlamp to counter the persistent darkness. I'd search for other lost souls who were poisoned with frustration and self-hatred. "Ignorance," I'd explain, "is the ultimate Walking Contradiction." You will catch it lurking in areas where it should not exist, although it will be absent where it's typically expected. It is also no coincidence that the first five letters of "ignorance" begin the word "ignore." People choose to ignore what they don't understand, not because they are evil. It is just easier . . .

It is not enough for me and other AS individuals to settle for "tolerance." Tolerance is just an unstable compromise between the neurotypical public and those individuals judged as . . . atypical. The neurotypical public hides behind the adage "live and let live," while making a conscious effort to not make our lives miserable. In return, the AS community accepts their place in the pecking order even though acceptance is sometimes the opiate of progress. I would leave the Trail and encourage my younger peers to flaunt the side of AS that can create outstanding friends, employees, students, coworkers, and even romantic partners. And someday, the DSM-IV will hopefully be revised to include the common traits of integrity and perseverance. On my popular online journal, I had confided about everything related to the Asperger's syndrome except the name of the actual disability itself. My pitiful excuse for not disclosing the AS was because it would pilfer attention from the Joey DiPaolo AIDS Foundation. In reality, I was just scared and not ready to invite such vulnerability. Now I was prepared to help destroy the disability stigma forever while advocating for those with more severe cases.

When my mother and father arrived at the hotel the next

morning, they were brandishing Mylar balloons and huge grins of relief. After seven months, they could finally stop worrying whether their only son was still safe in the woods, and also no longer had to worry about the psychological repercussions failure would have on me.

Sometime after my homecoming I would make the arrangements to travel to Disney World with a friend. We would ride the Haunted Mansion ride as we'd discussed, and as I had imagined all along the two-thousand-mile hike . . . and be mesmerized by the levitating candelabras while pretending not to notice the strings.

A FRACTURED FAIRY TALE

You can get so confused
that you'll start in to race
down long wiggled roads at a break-necking pace
and grind on for miles across weirdish wild space,
headed, I fear, toward a most useless place.
The Waiting Place . . .

—DR. SEUSS, *OH, THE PLACES YOU'LL GO!*

For at least three years after my hike ended, I was filled with such rage that I walked around with an occasional black eye from punching myself during spasms of frustration. Staring into a mirror had the effect of resurrecting painful memories followed by brief fits of self-abuse. My "weirdness" was no longer an asset I could use to justify myself, unlike when I was on the publicized 2,174-mile hike. A period of post-AT unemployment allowed me to get reacquainted with old *South Park* episodes (a crudely animated TV series featuring, among other things, an anthropomorphic bowel movement named Mr. Hankey). I squandered countless nights sloughing away brain cells with this recycled TV nonsense, occasionally taking a break to walk outside to urinate off the porch balcony—giggling as the golden arc disappeared into the illuminated charcoal moonlight. The neighbors undoubtedly caught me a few times, and must have come to the conclusion that our household plumbing was perpetually backed up.

Actually, my existence subsequent to my hike reminded me of a clogged toilet, with nostalgia as my only refuge. Entering adulthood can be traumatic for anyone, regardless of whether he or she suffers from a disability. For me, this difficult transition made me cling even more than usual to childhood memories. The luster and comfort of old Disney films began to fade when I noticed innuendo from repressed animators. One classic cartoon, for example, even insinuates that Goofy's wife was screwing the milkman, mailman, and a plethora of other servicemen, unbeknownst to her clueless husband.

By now, most of us have discovered the glory of YouTube (aka The Nostalgia Machine), which allows us to view any famous movie scene, musical number, or commercial with the touch of a computer key. Our cravings for "days of yore" also prompt us to flock to the formulaic movies that portray an adult protagonist making a fantastical return to school. We love movies like *17 Again* and *Never Been Kissed* because they exploit our collective desire for redemption . . . seizing back what we missed out on . . . and glossing over adolescent traumas.

With that redemptive do-over story arc in mind, I chose to live out this fantasy, or come as close to it as possible. After the post-hike lethargy finally dissipated, I signed up to be a substitute teacher in my old high school, so that I could be insulated by youth, predictability, and the talented teachers who had offered me support over the years. For a painfully brief period, I experienced the gift of constantly looking back and still seeing where I was going. But I was naive to believe substitute teaching would be a buffer for the transition into adulthood or would turn into an extension of my sometimes ideal high school years. In fact, it would ultimately feel like a medieval torture device.

Predictably, I had trouble maintaining some time-honored boundaries in the school setting. One day, in the presence of faculty and special education students, I began ranting about an episode of *Desperate Housewives* where a woman chose to breast-feed her four-year-old son in Lynette Scavo's advertising agency. Just as I was blurting out, "Oh, God! When the kid is old enough to ask for it . . . *it's time to stop!*" another teacher's hand pressed against my wrist. On another nonconsecutive occasion, a comment slipped out regarding Eva Longoria Parker. ("Gawd! Look at that chewin' gum walk! *Soooo* . . . WRIGLEY!") However, my favorite gaffe was repeating a line from *South Park* to quiet a rowdy class. ("Hey! This is a classroom. Not a Bangkok brothel.") Other times I made myself vulnerable for comments or gestures to be taken out of context, like when I winked at a young lady after pestering her for a hall pass. These lapses in conduct always came with consequences, as fear accelerated the maturity process. My professional survival would depend on constant vigilance, along with a willingness to take responsibility for my actions.

My old high school stopped calling for substitute teaching assignments when they began to see my inappropriate behavior as a liability. But I had previously been fired from every elementary and middle school in the entire district, despite deftly avoiding those minefields of the past. These terminations were not always provoked by my inappropriate behavior, but rather my noticeable struggle to control verbal shrapnel on the brink of spewing from my lips. Faculty and students judged me as nervous, awkward, uptight, or eccentric. One forthright student even confronted me: "After you first came to our school we saw no aura. You seemed to have no soul and just walked around like a zombie."

When the schools fired me, they communicated their decision by severing contact like a typical online date. In the meantime, I was left twiddling my thumbs for several weeks waiting for the phone to ring, instead of using this valuable time searching for new employment. One middle school principal was too lazy to make a two-minute phone call to the substitute teaching service, so he waited until I reported for duty before making up a lame excuse—twice. The teacher I was scheduled to replace had apparently experienced a dramatic convalescence or her recently deceased relative was no longer dead. My services were suddenly no longer needed.

One day, I finally confronted the grim reality that only $200 remained in my bank account, which was left over from a loan my father had given me. I searched the want ads in the *Poughkeepsie Journal*, but found nothing appropriate for someone with my skills and social deficiencies. To exacerbate my fall from grace, I surrendered to the twelve-hour night shifts at the IBM manufacturing plant that had hired me during all my college vacations and for a few months before my Appalachian Trail hike. The first check was rushed to the bank as though it were ancient parchment disintegrating with each fresh wave of oxygen. I wanted to burst into tears of relief as the bank teller made the deposit official. With every twelve-hour graveyard shift, I continued the arduous process of repairing my battered bank account and repaying my father one $50 bill at a time.

My kindest description of the IBM manufacturing complex is "Satan's Widget Factory." Every employee was put in charge of one robotic tool designed to process one tiny component of a complex, global machine. It took only two weeks for me to master the equipment and graduate to feeling a profound sense of alienation from no longer taking pride in my work. Stimulation came in the form of weekly checks, Red Bulls, the dining hall, and even coffee machines sputtering chemical sustenance. IBM's coffee always came out like glutinous sewage or lukewarm water quasi-diluted with coffee granules . . . although it *did* wake me up. YouTube nostalgia, unconditional support from family members, and my Disney CD collection ultimately stopped me from hanging myself with an extension cord. Tears sometimes spilled down my cheeks as I drove home—not from crying, but from staring. I feared a prolonged blink would put me asleep at the wheel . . . killing myself or someone else.

I was the only one of my coworkers with a college education, but did not put myself on a pedestal. These employees were, in actuality, heroes who had endured these grueling shifts for many years while battling life's unfair realities and their own demons. They were genuine fighters doing the absolute best they could. As I approached my fifteen-month anniversary at the IBM complex, their tolerance of my erratic personal hygiene and tendency to clean out my ears at the cafeteria tables began to wane. One night, I jeopardized my job by making a snide comment to my manager. Instead of using a napkin to wipe away food residue, she had the relentless habit of sucking her finger and making that accompanying "suction sound." Along with the sound of a nail clipper, "the finger-sucking thing" drives me more crazy than any other noise, reminding me of a tiny bomb detonated in increments of ninety seconds. One night, I lost patience and started to plead for mercy before a volcanic rage erupted inside her. I cowered until the tantrum was finally quelled and the bulging, purple vein receded back in her temple.

"How dare you?! How dare you insult me when most of what you do is just plain disgusting! I mean, you have been wearing the same shirt for the past two weeks! We don't want you sitting with us ever again."

My fellow staff members knew I had a case of "something," but they never asked questions. Unlike the people at my two previous jobs, they gave me a deserved "break" based on my redeeming Asperger's traits. For instance, I was meticulously punctual and seldom took a sick or personal day. I was one of the first employees to show up and the last one to leave. Some nights were tolerable because I listened to a five-disk collection of classic Disney while the 720 minutes melted away. Other nights were miserable . . . causing me to spout a dissonance of gibberish and obscenities. ("Fricking, gimlet-eyed, Scotchguard, motherfucking douche bag!") My coworkers sometimes caught me hitting myself, jumping up and down, or mumbling nonsense. Most of the time, they even gave me an *undeserved* break when I neglected bathing during the precious hour and a half of free time between sleeping and rushing back to work. Not only did I smell like rancid Stilton cheese, but I also neglected to change my clothes 90 percent of the time.

My best friend, Karl, was brutally honest about this severe lapse in personal hygiene. Genuine friendship, after all, should always revolve around honesty. "Jesse, you smell like a corpse!" he cried out. "I had to roll down the windows in your car!" The only time I made an earnest effort to clean myself up was when I had a date or went to a formal social gathering. Sometimes my own body odor even nauseated me!

I believe the last straw was when constant exposure to IBM's latex gloves provoked massive hive outbreaks. The discomfort was far more severe than poison ivy, except the angry boils would suddenly recede with no scarring. The only regions of my body spared were my face and—mercifully enough—my genitalia. Other bizarre ailments followed, such as groin fungus (possibly from not bathing) and a chemical burn on my tongue from nearly ingesting sodium hydroxide. The burn came from trying to consume a heart-shaped bar of soap that looked like Valentine's Day white chocolate. For ten days or so, mealtimes were sheer agony especially if foods contained ketchup. One night I lay facedown on the couch and overheard my sister loudly voicing her disgust in the other room.

"Will you please tell Jesse to get off the couch!? He never showers anymore."

My mother sighed. "Yeah, I know. But his life is very sad right now."

When not slaving away at my twelve-hour night-shift job, I faced rejection from countless women on a website called www .JDate.com. New York City harbors more Jewish women than the entire nation of Israel. All of them have rejected me. Most of the time, they didn't give a reason, and ignored me in hopes I would eventually get the message. The "reasons" (when I got them) always seemed unfair or beyond my control. It was either "You are really weird," "You reveal too much about yourself," "Your emails are too long," "You live too far," "It creeps me out how many other girls are your Facebook friends," "I am bisexual and involved with another woman," "You try too hard," "You're too uptight," "I've started seeing someone else," "I just ended a relationship and am not ready to start dating again," "I like you, but I have no romantic attraction toward you," "You make me uncomfortable," "I just don't understand you," or simply "You scare me." First impressions were taken to an extreme level, while social limitations I could never surpass were mocked. And furthermore, I passively raged against well-meaning friends suggesting I limit myself to women with autism. It was an insult when I knew how much I had to offer anyone who gave me a chance.

Reading Facebook profiles of friends and obscure acquaintances exacerbated my depression. They were getting married, breaking free from their parents' households, blazing career paths, starting romantic relationships, or finding a passion. Their successes were a stark contrast with my failures and aimless life.

It would be an exaggeration, however, to claim there were no highlights during this period of mediocrity. The happiest moments of this transitional period, as has so often been the case for me, occurred when I found myself the center of attention or entertained an audience in some capacity. My public clowning once occurred on the Metro-North train after yet another disastrous online date. A gaggle of young ladies were loudly arguing over a game of Trivial Pursuit while the other passengers watched in amusement. Another question came along. "What movie did Ben Affleck and Matt Damon first star in together?"

When they cried out, *Good Will Hunting*, I interjected, "Oh, God! You are *all* wrong! It was actually *School Ties*! You see, Ben Affleck and Matt Damon grew up together! They attended the same school and acted in *School Ties* before cowriting the *Good Will Hunting* screenplay. In *School Ties* Matt Damon played the role of the boy who falsely accuses Brendan Fraser of cheating. Ben Affleck only had a minor role."

One thing led to another until all of sudden, I had an audience, and I launched into a monologue about my blind dates that came prepackaged with doom. (I always believed the term "blind date" implied you wanted to gouge out your eyes with a prison shiv and stumble through the rest of the evening without looking at your date.)

I stood up and boisterously rose to the occasion as the caboose comedian. The miscellaneous audience ranged from a seventy-year-old widow to a thirty-something-year-old couple who'd just seen *Jersey Boys* on Broadway. The laughter of strangers had the psychotropic effect of absolving my unhappiness and my "online dating monologue" sugarcoated the misogynistic contempt I had for women at the time. They were insincere, selfish, unforgiving, inconsiderate, manipulative, flakey, fickle, and cruel. The late George Carlin once said that buying a puppy is like purchasing a small tragedy. You love something that you know will die a slow, agonizing death in a relatively short period of time. The same concept may be applicable toward romantic relationships, which are budding pustules of disaster. I mean, let's face the facts: You either stay together until one half of the partnership passes away or the romance is eventually terminated by one party. But why did women choose to end romantic relationships at the worst possible times? The heartbreaks they caused always seemed to coincide with job terminations, the holiday season, Valentine's Day, deaths of family members, school dances, or planned vacations. Women appeared to leech nutrients from male tears, and I nursed this anger without considering its irrationality or how women share the same grievances about their male counterparts. Or how I was probably guilty of the same infractions and was thus a *hyppocwit*. I hated women for the simple reason that they constantly reminded me of how different I was.

I consciously trampled the damn eggshells and didn't mind when the conductor griped, "Will you please keep your voice down? I can hear you from the other car and other passengers are complaining!" I no longer cared, especially when the thirty-year-old couple came up to me afterward and said, "We are probably going to remember this train ride for the rest of our lives!" A few weeks later I would cross paths with the female half of this couple at the Pleasant Valley Post Office, where she opened up about raising two autistic children. It was not necessary to confide about my Asperger's syndrome because she already knew.

"After we said good-bye to you, I said to my boyfriend, 'I really hope that is my son in fifteen years.'"

The African adage "It takes a village to raise a child" never actually ends for someone with a disability. Even as an adult, I found critical relationships among people in my community who tolerated and even admired my uniqueness. These human connections blossomed at the bank . . . post office . . . and the Daily Planet (not the fictional newspaper in Superman's Metropolis, but a popular diner located across the street from my old high school).

The Daily Planet quickly became a sanctuary where I could depend on the quirky ambience and its perpetually cheerful staff. The walls were festooned with antique radios, 1950s movie posters, and *New York Times* articles chronicling major events of the last century, such as the moon landing and Nixon's resignation. Television sets, suspended from the ceiling, played grainy commercials from an era when owning a TV was a luxury enjoyed by affluent Americans. And if you spent enough time at the Daily Planet, you would probably catch Ronald Reagan hawking dishwashing detergent or a leathery cowboy advertising cigarettes.

The restaurant's power had the effect of glossing over the shameful moments of America's last century, sealing it inside a steel-plated lunch box forever. It is a symbol for hope and stability even when it seems like the rest of the world is collapsing.

At the Daily Planet, it is common for me and other men in the

Asperger's community to be bombarded with attention from gorgeous, flirtatious women. Sometimes they even sit with us to strike up a conversation, wanting to know more about our dateless, socially maladjusted lives. We live for the moments when they give us a hug or caress our shoulder. Unfortunately, these "relationships" are artificially sustained by an exchange of money in the form of tips. The dynamics of these relationships abruptly change when I misconstrue this attention as an invitation for a full-blown friendship or even a romantic connection. As opposed to prolonging the awkwardness, the young woman sensibly chooses to terminate contact when I begin showing up with the occasional rose or birthday card. Her once-effervescent personality dwindles to a forced smile. Blanche, the composite of all sweet, albeit homely, diner waitresses, is assigned to take over my table because "Amber" is supposedly too inundated with other customers every time. But it was different with Jessy. The Daily Planet was different . . .

By my mid-twenties, I had matured enough to understand that the attention of a flirtatious and/or friendly staff is not necessarily an invitation for a romantic relationship. But as the Daily Planet evolved into a family-friendly Hooters, I became particularly attached to a young waitress named Jessy—a former runway model and doppelganger of Jennifer Lopez—who inspired me to keep going. Our relationship was more complex than the typical customer/waitress small talk, as Jessy took an unusually strong interest in my endeavors. I do not know if she specifically identified me as having mild autism, but Jessy did judge me to possess an enigmatic force that could radiate benevolence if given a chance. When I confided about my desire to write a book, she replied with her usual enthusiasm, "Oh, yeah! You should write about, you know . . . your struggles! When you first came in here, you seemed depressed. I could tell something was very different. Something special." Jessy felt comfortable asking me personal questions. In return, I felt comfortable asking her out on a date at intervals of eight months to a year without worrying about stalking accusations followed by police involvement. It was an extremely fair barter . . .

WEIRDISH ROMANCE

I have always wondered what it would feel like to be a celebrity, and I spent most of my childhood nursing these fantasies. But my desire did not stem from a lust for wealth and power. I simply wanted to be "liked" without dealing with the repercussions of Asperger's syndrome. The disastrous first impressions would come to an abrupt halt, as the public judged me on my thespian talents—the legendary roles, my charitable contributions, and the millions of lives I touched through the mass mediums of television, newspaper, Internet, and cinema. The innate "weirdness" would be justified and glossed over by a lifetime of intense overcompensation. And most important, women would naturally gravitate toward me. Any preconceived illusions about celebrity lifestyles were finally altered after meeting an actor at a conclave for Reform Jewish youths in January 1999.

I had never heard of him before our respective universes collided, but I was starstruck along with everybody else. At age seventeen, the actor had been a main character on a popular TV show, where he played a nerdy high school student. He was arguably the nation's youngest, most successful stand-up comic at the time. His geeky persona made it easier for directors to typecast him as the socially challenged nerd. But he only pretended to be a dweeb on TV and was a celebrity in real life. Therefore, I assumed he was liberated from the consistent social and romantic rejections that had always affected my life. During the bus ride back to the synagogue in Rockland County, New York, another teenager pressed the actor about all the women he must score on a regular basis. He sighed as he answered, "Oh, yeah. I get hit on by girls constantly. But they are girls who have not even had their Bat Mitzvahs yet!"

He continued, "I had a really low moment the other week while watching *Sally Jessy Raphael*. They had a group of brothers on the show who have that genetic condition causing them to grow thick black hair all over their bodies. They are called the 'Wolfmen.' Anyway, I see them on the show with the most gorgeous blondes I have ever seen! I thought to myself, 'How is it possible these guys can get girls like that? But I have, um . . . let's see. Nobody!'"

My kindred geek heart went out to the poor guy after he finished the soliloquy. For the first time all weekend, we were not divided by his television stardom. I related to his anecdote and had experienced my own epiphany of anguish just a few weeks earlier while watching the movie *Mask*.

Mask is the inspirational story of a severely deformed teenager named Rocky Dennis (played by an unrecognizable Eric Stoltz under pounds of prosthetic makeup). Initially, his new junior high school classmates recoil in horror, until Rocky quickly wins them over with his effervescent wit and intelligence. The turning point comes when Rocky meets a beautiful teenage girl while volunteering at a camp for the blind. Because his new girl-friend is visually impaired, she does not judge or even care about Rocky's deformity. At that point in the film, I chose to run around the house, flapping my hands in despair while screaming, "You see!? Even *that* guy has a girlfriend. And *I don't!*"

My family laughed at the circus tantrum. But for me, the silliness was just a mask for the pain.

I had not seen the last of the actor when that weekend ended. He made cameos in popular sitcoms over the years and starred in an online comedy that focused on doomed romantic endeavors. The socially challenged characters he portrayed always made me feel better about my own shortcomings and the fathomless abyss of what I would never understand about women.

My first lesson on women was taught by the glossy pages of the libido-placating, erection-causing, fantasy-inducing, unrealistic-expectations-building pages of *Playboy* magazine. I discovered the stack of my father's chronologically filed magazines in the basement of my old house, among the loose eight-track tapes and the vinyl records lined with wispy cobwebs. I could not help myself, because even a trained Seeing Eye dog cannot contain himself when red meat is dangled in front of his nasal passages.

These particular magazines immediately forged my standards of physical attraction in the worst way. I registered beauty only in those women endowed with grapefruit breasts capped with sensuous, erect nipples. There must have been some *Playboy* centerfolds who also had high IQs and enough intellectual caliber to become doctors. But who cared? Everything above the breasts seemed to make no difference as long as it was a beautiful face.

And to put it as tactfully as possible, those theories of blindness and hairy palms were proven to be erroneous through my daily habits. An old wives' tale, if you will. If these superstitions had even a modicum of truth, I would have transformed into a near-sighted, humanoid Sasquatch by age fourteen. Perhaps my father knew what was going on, so he decided to have a talk with me one day.

"This is not the way real women look, Jesse," he sighed. "It is just a fantasy and nothing more. Even the *Playboy* models probably do not look like that. It is all airbrushed and you do not even see any beauty marks. And even if you did end up with a woman who looks like that, chances are she would be a real pain in the ass."

A child with high-functioning autism is going to face a life-time of social obstacles. But for me, no challenge has been more tenacious than my romantic pursuits.

The common saying "Women are a labyrinth" has always been a gross understatement for me, because the journey seemed more like an Indiana Jones maze infested with deadly booby traps. My attempts to initiate conversation have often been con-strued as creepy and/or overbearing. And genuine compliments have been perceived as insults.

"Hey, Andrea! What's up? I hope you have been enjoying your semester so far, and I've been meaning to tell you some-thing. I think you ought to have an alias and have come up with the perfect one. From this moment on, you will be known as 'The Composite.' It's just that you remind me of *so* many people I've known throughout my life whose names I *just can't* think of right now!"

I wait for her to smile and say, "I get that all the time! Who do I remind you of?" Instead, her upper lip curls in annoyance as she replies in flamboyant sarcasm, "Oh, God! I find that to be just *so* interesting! Especially considering you have only met me like . . . twice in your entire life! You know, I have always considered myself to be very unique!"

That's not to say hope was totally nonexistent.

My father often brags how total strangers used to stop him in airports and hotel lobbies just to tell him how beautiful my sister and I were. I was a good-looking child growing up, and people padded my fragile self-esteem with genuine compliments to compensate for the insults. Comments about my "beautiful brown eyes" were frequent, and girls would sometimes gravitate toward this feature. Even during squalls of acne, braces, glasses, and an oversized nose, my handsomeness somehow endured. At a teenage nightclub, a young woman shyly handed me a dollar bill with her phone number on it. And when I attended my cousin Patrick's Bar Mitzvah as a twenty-year-old college sophomore, my sister gave me a rare glimpse into the porcelain grotto known as the Women's Bathroom. Vicariously experiencing it through Dena's ears, the flighty banter warmed me.

"God! *Who is he!?* He is, like, the only cute guy in this entire place! But he is kind of weird. I mean, most people do not try to meet girls at someone's Bar Mitzvah."

Let's face it. Looks are not everything, but they sure as hell can help! Beauty is always in the eye of the beholder, although it was comforting to know that some women would find me physically attractive. These flattering gestures planted the seeds of confidence and optimism for the future.

My quasi-good looks led to plenty of infatuations, which were precipitously halted once my female suitor detected something was a little . . . off. Her phone calls and emails would end, as she always sent the message by "ignoring me." Perhaps I would someday gloss over some of the superficial weirdness that had always been a catalyst for rejection. I nursed this hope like the hint of flame lingering in the black hollow of a menorah branch, grasping at tiny wax particles to sustain life for a few more seconds. My endless streak of romantic failures would finally come to an abrupt halt when two fantastical realities entered my life: *Desperate Housewives* and Linda.

The premise of the television show *Desperate Housewives* is how many women do not lose their beauty (and capacity for erotic shenanigans) as their youth begins to fade. With the exception of Gabrielle Solis (Eva Longoria Parker), all of the women are well past their forties and wreak havoc in a fictional California neighborhood called Wisteria Lane. Despite the occasional statutory rape, murder, suicide, arson, and tornado, the women of Wisteria Lane pushed onward every Sunday night at 9 p.m. And I developed an Annie Wilkes–like fixation on the faux neighborhood the way an uber-nerd scrutinizes a *Star Trek* website. Furthermore, it is impossible not to become obsessed with a show whose pilot episode features a seventeen-year-old gardener seduced by the older, married woman down the street. But not just any woman. His seducer is a former Manhattan fashion model played by an actress considered to be one of the most beautiful women in the world. The plotlines grew so stimulating that I would often use commercial breaks to flap my hands in another room.

Shortly after *Desperate Housewives* entered my life, on a singles' hiking expedition, I struck up a conversation with a ninth-grade English teacher who was a mirror image of Demi Moore. From day one, I was not bothered by the fact that Linda was forty and I happened to be only twenty-two. The universe was cognizant that I had suffered for too long and was long overdue for the cosmos to align in my favor. A supernatural phenomenon of solar storms and heavenly meteor showers would rain upon my life for just a little while.

I told friends, family members, acquaintances, and near strangers about my romance with Linda. They wanted to know whether Linda had mental problems, and I sometimes asked myself the same question. If she were actually engulfed by a mental challenge, I could only pray the illness raged for as long as possible. My best friend, Karl, lampooned her age by inquiring whether she had died in my arms during intimacy. Another friend gingerly asked, "Um, in retrospect, did you feel that Linda was, you know . . . just *using you*?"

I replied, "Yes, I did get that impression. But under these particular circumstances I did not mind too much. If you know what I mean?" She understood and mercifully did not force me to elaborate.

The only people who were morbidly supportive of my dalliance with an eighteen-years-older, non-Jewish woman were my parents. The degree of comfort and approval they demonstrated surprised and even sort of mortified me. One afternoon I left the house for one of my "visits" with Linda. As I was halfway out the door, I announced to my mother that I would be stopping at the CVS pharmacy. She put her fingers to her mouth to stifle a gasp and whispered, "Oh, my God. Have you run out of condoms?" On another equally disturbing occasion, I asked my mother why she and my father had not seemed to have any qualms about me dating a much older, gentile woman. I'm not sure she even blinked when she answered, "Well . . . we knew you probably would not end up marrying her. We just wanted you to get *laid*!" Both of these nauseating moments turned my hands into sentient appendages. They flapped violently, as though attempting to flee the shackles of my wrists.

"No! No! NOOOOOO!" I screamed. Flap . . . flap . . . flap. Flap!

Thus was the beautiful routine of the first few months of my post-college life. I padded my bank account with enormous paychecks from an IBM manufacturing plant, indulged in my letter-writing/postal obsession, was free from seventeen consecutive years of grueling academia, and made the weekly hour-long drive to have passionate adventures with Linda, who also could not comprehend the universe's magnanimity. "It feels like I have won the lottery," she purred. "I think you are an *incredible* man." It was impossible to ignore or downplay my new, beautifully skewed realities. Realities that seemed nearly fictional.

Linda was not my first experience with sex, although my first time is nothing to be nostalgic about. I always treated my virginity like a case of poison sumac, which could be banished with one panacea. Therefore, I offered my virginity to the first heavyset woman willing to take it, during my 2003 study abroad program in Bath, England. The young lady was a year older as well as a complete stranger I had met only fifteen minutes earlier at a seedy nightclub. Once the room's lighting was restored and residual alcohol was metabolized by my liver, any initial attraction ceased to exist. The sex was void of intimacy, but took away much of the shame that came with lack of experience. It also took away the fear of a woman never taking an interest in me as "more than a friend."

Dating Linda was liberating because I no longer had to monitor what came out of my mouth every microsecond. Like the bowels of a long-dormant volcano, I let nonsense bubble from my mouth to fill precarious, awkward silences.

"You know, Linda. While studying in Bath, England, I was watching a documentary called *Fat Girls and Feeders*. It featured a subculture of men who have an intense sexual attraction toward grotesquely obese women. It is like the wires are crossed in their brains or something! One man's wife was so obese that they needed a cattle pulley just to get her out of bed. And her husband thought she was the sexiest woman he had ever met!"

I braced for the standard eye-rolling due to the randomness, stupidity, and insensitivity of my comments. But it never came with Linda. She always responded with intellectual enthusiasm. She was the first woman who took a long-term interest in me while allowing me to be myself.

Linda's beautiful daughter, Tiffany, was six years younger than me and had an adult boyfriend. I got the impression that, like me, he was trying to compensate in adulthood for social shortcomings that had robbed him of the chance to form age-appropriate relationships throughout his life. And also like me, he was a twenty-two-year-old named Jesse. It was at that moment when I knew my life had truly taken on the fantastical potency of a *Desperate Housewives* episode.

Linda would shimmer for a little while before fading away as breathtaking things always do. In the meantime, I preferred to downplay the realities of my romance. The woman admitted she had not had sex for the better part of the decade, which can lead to drastically lowered standards. And finally, Linda would eventually grow bored with me. One night in November 2004, I was more preoccupied with watching *The Simpsons* Halloween special at a bar than conversing with her. She was so quiet as we walked toward the car that I had a grim premonition of what was coming next.

When Linda dumped me four months into our relationship, just a few days before Thanksgiving, I accepted her decision with unusual class. I, the King of Perseveration, am famous for pushing against any romantic rejection that I deem to be premature or unfair. Maybe someday I will accept one inalienable truth about the feminine species: When a woman makes up her mind, trying to change it is about as effective as using a fine-tooth comb to saw through a wood knot.

The Linda Experience made me entertain the possibility of settling into a comfortable niche as a long-term, unpaid gigolo for attractive older women like her. Women who have been repeatedly thrashed about by a vindictive Cupid and have almost given up on romance. Yes! I would deliriously run off into the night searching for more Lindas who had been scarred by sexual frustration, disastrous marriages, and philandering husbands who ran away with someone younger and arguably more attractive. Like Linda, these women would overlook my social ineptitude and focus on the qualities that should matter the most: integrity, reliability, punctuality . . . a twenty-something libido. I would fly into bedrooms like an adult tooth fairy, to satisfy women in their late thirties to early forties facing the looming threat of middle age. I would also settle for being paraded around at weddings, Bar Mitzvahs, communions, funerals, and other functions where she knew we would cross paths with her former husband as well as his younger and pregnant new wife. But when my new companion felt she had made her point, I would be unceremoniously "dumped" until the next opportunity to be flaunted like a dancing bear. But my other alternatives (it seemed) were involuntary celibacy or failing to understand the mind games commonplace with younger mates. Of course, the occasional critic would sneer at my conquests while condemning me as a joke . . . a gullible tool void of dignity. But I would be content.

Linda severed all contact, as people typically do after terminating a romantic connection. (The "let's still be friends" line is a hybrid between a pleasant lie and crock of shit.). "Linda" for me is a term that now alludes to those brief gaps of time when the social repercussions of Asperger's would wane just enough for the veil of perpetual weirdness to stop being a negative. Every individual with AS needs to experience at least one "Linda." Her essence lingers in my life as a metaphor, a glimmer of hope shimmering above a Sea of Hopelessness.

LISTIES

For the most part, my life exists in the form of an enormous list. The best lists are the ones whose contents serve as a means to an end. It is these lists, which provide me with a sense of duty . . . tasks defining a day yet to be seized. My lists also become the perfect weapons to justify procrastination, as they radiate the illusion of productivity. My father once told me, "You are the busiest person I know who hardly gets anything done." Most important, they give me a sense of order and predictability in a world that has anything but.

For example . . .

HALLOWEEN LIST

- Purchase rotund pumpkins at Adams Fairacre Farms and buy a book of jack-o'-lantern carving patterns. Carve out all the smallest orifices (windows, doors) first when using the Haunted House pattern.

- Take a trip to the Pleasant Valley Copy Shack to enlarge jack-o'-lantern patterns to fit the girth of my pumpkins and make carving less cumbersome.

- Give $95 to the mall's Halloween store for the Beetlejuice suit and face mask.

- Draft a standard letter to all the families in my neighborhood explaining that I paid $75 for my costume and am devoting two days to carving jack-o'-lanterns from the most complicated patterns. Gingerly explain that I hope they will visit my house and admire the jack-o'-lanterns, with or without small children. Also try to squeeze in something about the Asperger's syndrome to further justify my actions.

- Watch the ancient VHS copy of Walt Disney's Bing Crosby–narrated *Legend of Sleepy Hollow* while exercising stark naked on the elliptical trainer downstairs when nobody is home. Avoid posting this "status" on Facebook because my parents found out about it last time while they were vacationing in Europe.

- Watch the *Disney Halloween Treats* special on YouTube while writing an email to Katie, who I met last week on www .JDate.com (a site for Jewish people who cannot find romantic relationships due to unappealing physical appearance and/or personality, poor personal hygiene, manic codependency, children from a previous relationship, and of course, Asperger's syndrome). Send a new email ten days later if she fails to write back. Send a third email ten days after that asking if she wishes to remain in contact and to please give me the courtesy of letting me know. Then let it go . . .

- Write an email to my supervisor at the funeral home and remind them that I am unable to work on Friday, October 30, and Saturday, October 31, because of my Halloween preparations. It is in poor taste to have wake services on Halloween anyway.

- Locate the CD of scary Halloween noises and set up the stereo close to the front door.

- Make my fourth appointment this month to donate a bag of platelets at the IBM Blood Center to receive a $50 gift card. Disregard how the amount of gas required to make the hour round-trip four times in a month is roughly equivalent to the gift card.

In my fantasies, the eyes of my fellow neighbors are shimmering with tears after I hand them my Halloween letter. They are touched that a grown man would invest so much time and money toward building Halloween memories for their children. The matriarch is also contemplating inviting me to their house for dinner, where I'll regale the table with perfectly appropriate family-friendly anecdotes. But the delusions of grandeur always pass over me like a wave. It is more probable that a frantic housewife is checking the sex offender registry to see if a crimson dot shows up at my address, as Junior applies the finishing touches to his Charlie Chaplin makeup. She will find nothing on the website, but she'll still say to her child, "Why don't we skip that brown-and-white house? You'll still have enough candy to last until next spring!" But I'd like to believe a small handful of families might give my Halloween rituals a chance.

I persist with my Asperger's silliness, but approximately 50 percent of the time I maintain a firm grip on reality. People will come to their own judgments, which will often be caustic, and reality has an entirely different agenda from our own. But I hope for the best.

Sometimes I dream about making another list even though some of its items would probably remain uncrossed . . . perhaps forever.

ASPERGER'S LIST

• Petition the major American psychiatric associations to revise the DSM-IV to include more of the redeeming symptoms of Asperger's instead of the "negative traits," which usually warrant psychiatric intervention. (Integrity, reliability, and honesty must be heavily emphasized. Someday the stereotype will evolve in the other direction, as people start to think of us after losing their wallets or purses in New York City. They can do nothing else except hope it ends up in the hands of someone with AS.)

• Create a reoccurring Asperger's character who is a composite of the late Jim Varney's Ernest P. Worrell, the late John Candy, and the late Andy Kaufman (who is believed to have had AS). Let him forever serve as the underdog comic foil who ultimately rises to the occasion to save the day.

- Eliminate ignoring as a form of communication in American culture when so many of our problems can be solved by being just a little more confrontational.

- Force American elementary schools to demonstrate the same tolerance toward substitute teachers with an autism spectrum disorder as they do to their learning-disabled students.

- Draft a memorandum to any woman I dare ask out on a date who works within a local store or restaurant. Explain that my well-meaning actions are not a precursor for stalking. And, just because I'm really weird, I still have the right to ask someone if they want to meet me at Starbucks.

- Identify all Hollywood actors with prominent Asperger's symptoms and hound them night and day with letters and/or emails until one of them "comes out of the closet."

- Embark on a hike of the 2,600-plus-mile Pacific Crest Trail, which stretches from Mexico to Canada. Hike for pediatric autism and give 90 percent of the proceeds to the organization while maintaining a daily online blog.

- Create a social service organization responsible for obtaining employment for individuals with Asperger's syndrome.

- Pitch a new show to the TV networks, in which a strikingly beautiful, neurotypical former runway model must choose between twenty very eligible bachelors. All of them live with Asperger's syndrome and have not been out on more than five dates in their entire lives.

SPEAKING OUT

Don't tell when you're angry. Try instead to tell when you feel
strong, or when you're feeling good about who you are.

—MICHAEL JOHN CARLEY,
ASPERGER'S FROM THE INSIDE OUT

Knowing when and whom to tell about my diagnosis has been
the most treacherous part of my journey. I tend to agree with the
autism activist and author Michael John Carley when he advises,
"You should tell when it feels safe." My parents and I, however,
did not often feel safe. Certain loved ones continued to believe
that my monotone voice was merely a speech impediment—
something that should be corrected. Other relatives attributed
my mediocre jobs to a lack of ambition or lingering perseveration over the completed Appalachian Trail hike. A great-aunt
once muttered over the phone, "Is that the best you can do?" It
was hard to shake the fear that these skeptical observers would
dismiss the diagnosis as yet another excuse, or an attempt to
jump on the bandwagon of pop psychology.

A negative reaction may come from a generational gap, lack

of empathy toward mild disabilities, or simply because the uncle/
aunt/third cousin/etc. is an asshole. But some relatives will reject
a diagnosis for another reason. Having an open mind forces
them to confront painful memories of how they may have judged
the challenges within their own children. For this particular reason, my mother decided never to tell my maternal grandfather,
even though my grandmother always knew. We lost the option
to "disclose" as Alzheimer's atrophied his mind. Perhaps we
should have trusted him to understand and not assumed he
would have misjudged my uniqueness as he may have done with
his own son. My uncle definitely had one or two skeletons in his
closet . . . *literally*.

I was fortunate enough to have Uncle Justin in my life, even
though Las Vegas seemed like seven light-years away. During my
sister's and my childhood, he was incredibly attentive to us, while
arguably being responsible for my lifelong Disney obsession.
Around my sixth birthday, an enormous box arrived at my doorstep. I plundered through the packing peanuts to salvage three
treasures—a VHS tape of *Sleeping Beauty* nestled between an
animatronic Mickey Mouse and Goofy. The characters, complete
with intermittent blinking, told a story once a cassette was
shoved in their asses. Both the VHS tape and the mechanical
reincarnations of these Disney icons were cutting-edge novelties
in the mid-1980s and filled me with the same intoxicating wonder as YouTube would two decades later. Uncle Justin was a
lovable hybrid of Peter Pan and Joey Gladstone from *Full
House*—he breathed magic into my childhood. As an adult, however, I reminisce about his eccentricities and wonder if he lived
with an undiagnosed disability.

The last time I saw Uncle Justin was more than ten years ago,
during a family vacation in Las Vegas. I walked into his apart-

ment for the first time, which reminded me of an abandoned warehouse. Boxes of computer games were piled everywhere, covered in a film of dust and newspaper flakes. I look back on this scene as a sad Museum of Inertia—artifacts of a confused life. Crammed among the debris was an antique Vegas slot machine as well as a primitive arcade game, Spaced Invaders. He gestured to a Halloween decoration slumped between two shelves that were swollen with phonebook-size computer manuals.

"Do you like my skeleton, Jesse?"

"Yeah! It is pretty cool! What store did you buy it from?"

Uncle Justin replied, "I ordered it from India in some catalog. It is a real human skeleton!"

"What do you mean?" I asked.

He explained, "I sent away for a dead human being and assembled its bones in my apartment. I used to hang it inside the bathroom to scare one of my old girlfriends when she used the toilet in the middle of the night. The first time it happened, she actually peed on the floor! But now I have a lot more respect for Billy and have stopped using him to play pranks anymore."

As if to validate his flamboyant oddness, Uncle Justin proceeded to show me the catalog from which he had ordered the arid remains (that he had apparently named). They had once walked the earth as a vibrant human being and could not have anticipated spending the first few years of eternity hanging out in Uncle Justin's dusty apartment. I played Spaced Invaders, experienced my first Gambler's Rush when silver change poured from the slot machine, and became ecstatic when Uncle Justin handed me a CD-ROM of *Jesus vs. Frosty*, the crudely animated short that led to the creation of *South Park*. I had been trying for weeks to access the cartoon during those days before high-speed Internet and YouTube. Downloading a seven-minute video entailed leaving my damn terminal on all night long, until cyber-traffic usually aborted the process.

My mother had known about my diagnosis for over a year when she made the decision to confide in her brother during this vacation. Uncle Justin expressed concern and admitted, "I could see he is struggling with something." If only he could see me in the present . . .

Shortly after being terminated from substitute teaching, I returned to my old high school to deliver a presentation at a teach-in, a series of morning lectures revolving around one specific theme: intolerance. While walking toward the podium, I scanned the audience compiled of doppelgangers—ghostly composites of former classmates. Everybody was there. The football heroes; achingly beautiful girls provoking synchronized head-turning from male admirers; malicious bullies preying on the weak and/or socially naive; apathetic burnouts who barely came to school three days a week; and overachievers responsible beyond their years. Somewhere in the Adolescent Ocean were those students whose high school experience was saturated with profound loneliness. The personalities will never change, although they are now accessorized with jewel-encrusted iPods and portable DVD players.

"Hello, my name is Jesse Saperstein. I am a 2000 graduate of Arlington High School, and majored in English at Hobart and William Smith Colleges. About two and a half years ago, I decided to attempt a hike of the Appalachian Trail from Georgia to Maine. I walked for 2,174 miles, and it took me seven months to finish. Not only did I complete my hike, but I succeeded in raising at least $19,000 for a pediatric AIDS foundation.

"I am not telling you this to brag, but to let you know I accomplished all this with a disability. I have the mildest, most misunderstood, form of autism, known as Asperger's syndrome."

My words stumbled out like drunken circus harlequins as I repeated the contents of a popular email forward.

"Let's fast-forward to the future," I began. "The year is 2016—time for a brand-new presidential election with exciting new candidates the world has never seen before. There are three candidates competing for the Democratic nomination. And here they are.

"The first candidate is physically handicapped and is often in poor health. He chain-smokes and is a borderline alcoholic. He bases his decisions on the advice of astrologists and associates with crooked politicians. This candidate has also had countless extramarital affairs.

"The second candidate is not much better than the last one. He is obese and is also an alcoholic. He is also legendary for his socially inappropriate behavior when intoxicated. One time a high-society woman confronted him to say, 'Dear, God, sir! You are drunk!' He replied, 'That may be so, but by tomorrow I'll be sober. And you'll still be ugly!' His laziness causes him to sleep until noon every single day, with no exercise. He is learning disabled with either dyslexia or attention deficit disorder.

"And now . . . the third candidate!" I cried out. "The third candidate is a decorated war hero and a talented painter. He is also a gifted orator, a nice guy, never drinks except one beer on occasion, and is kind to both women and children. He cherishes animals and is passionate about vegetarianism. Most important, the third candidate almost always does everything he says he is going to do.

"All of us will probably vote for the third candidate. Won't we?" Titters of agreement fill the room. "But what we do not know is the first candidate is Franklin Delano Roosevelt. The second candidate is Winston Churchill. And the third, flawless candidate is none other than . . . Adolf Hitler!

"It kind of makes you guys think twice before judging somebody . . . doesn't it?"

The oration turned serious as I opened up to the students about how it feels living with Asperger's syndrome—a silent disability prematurely condemned as a character defect, with too many doomed first impressions.

> *If we look at AS through a different lens,*
> *though, we can reframe some of these "deficits"*
> *as assets. Because an individual with AS is*
> *unfettered by the chains of social convention*
> *or "manners," he may be able to identify*
> *unique solutions that no one else notices.*
>
> —TERESA BOLICK, *ASPERGER SYNDROME AND*
> *ADOLESCENCE: HELPING PRETEENS AND TEENS GET*
> *READY FOR THE REAL WORLD*

Over the next few years, my public speaking evolved. The humor turned mildly risqué in order to appeal to a broader spectrum of listeners:

We all have a little trouble filtering what comes out of our mouths. Even people who should know better and foresee the severe consequences . . . make mistakes. According to a popular legend, Groucho Marx allegedly came close to destroying his television career when chatting with a guest about his family.

"Yes, sir! I have eight children."

"Dear God! How did you end up with eight children?!"

"What can I say?" the man sighed. "I love my wife."

"Oh, yeah? Well, I love my cigar! But I still take it out once in a while!"

People with Asperger's syndrome have a difficult time controlling what comes out of their mouths, and stuff like this tends to happen to them *all the time*. Despite this common challenge, most individuals with AS are just as incredible and unique as anyone else. They could come across as overly polite, rude, mellow, angry, passive, aggressive, passive-aggressive, shy, gregarious, learning disabled, or a freaking genius! Regardless of how you describe each individual, there is usually something about them that is, um . . . a little different.

My first professional gig took place at a Minnesota private school in December 2008. Long-distance traveling always makes me feel vulnerable, as though a sadist has crammed a cluster of peeled bananas down my pants before shoving me into a chimpanzee sanctuary. My nostrils flare and my eyes fixate toward my crotch while I wait for the inevitable. But maybe things will work out if I just remain calm and inconspicuous. My travel-related humor ("I hear this is the flight where all the families are heading to the Convention for Colicky Infants!") is unappreciated and can eventually lead to trouble.

When bad weather canceled my Minnesota flight, I hopped rides to two other airports in search of a flight as my travel nightmare continued. Driving to three airports in the space of a few hours earned me an automatic ranking on the "Suspected Terrorist List." At the third airport, a team of security guards promptly escorted me away to rifle through my belongings. (A similar encounter happened four years earlier when I absentmindedly wore my Israeli army hat on a train heading toward the 2004 Republican National Convention, on my way home from visiting a college friend in Maryland. After the transit detective completed his FBI background check, he exclaimed, "What were you thinking?! Didn't someone warn you about wearing a hat like this in public? In this day and age?" The only positive aspect of these random encounters is the authorities' insistence on carrying my belongings. I smile and pretend they are my entourage.) Unlike some of my neurotypical peers, I am as courteous to them as they are to me and understand that the day's suffering will be alleviated by my willingness to cooperate.

Every speech I give is slightly tweaked depending on the audience, but the message is always the same. We live in a society where first impressions are taken to a level of severe and sometimes ridiculous importance. Society is always watching . . . forever judging . . . and relentlessly criticizing. Our celebrities have it particularly rough in their fishbowl existence, and they do not receive many breaks. Despite all the other issues deserving media attention, we choose to dwell on our First Lady allegedly breaking monarchial protocol by putting her hand on Queen Elizabeth's shoulder. Sometimes I fantasize about becoming the first (and last) Jewish president of the United States. In reality, however, I am man enough to respect my limitations and acknowledge I would become the veritable U.S. President from Hell. My constant gaffes would give the media a field day several times a week:

"President Saperstein Caught Scratching His Testicles in Public."

"Saperstein Farts While Speaking at United Nations Summit in Geneva—Tries to Cover It Up by Loudly Coughing."

"President Saperstein Under Fire Again! Tells Inappropriate Anecdote About Marx Brother Groucho to Public School Children."

My audience's applause turns into an auditory narcotic and the twenty- to thirty-minute time constraints are not enough to elaborate on *just taking another look* . . . Take another look at yourselves, your misfit peers, and even your legendary cultural icons.

What you see on the movie or TV screen, or in the glossy magazines, doesn't tell the whole story about the real lives and challenges that even the most famous and powerful face. Whether they're brawny action-movie stars, successful entrepreneurs, long-time television personalities, or other bold-faced names, chances are that some have grappled with learning disabilities, developmental delays, phobias, and other problems—perhaps in even greater proportion than the general public.

Unusually successful people are not necessarily those benefiting from the Genetic Lottery of physiology, intelligence, and raw talent. Their victories are engineered through sheer determination or choosing life paths that test their vulnerabilities. They are the unsung heroes who constantly bite the unfair hand life has dealt them. Like me, they choose to reject the Opiate of the Cynical Masses. "Life is just not fair. Get used to it!"

If you like what you see on this stage . . . I ask that you take the admiration you have toward me and extend it toward your peers who struggle with disabilities. Or maybe those peers who do not even have a diagnosed disability. Perhaps there is nothing wrong with them except being downright weird. But maybe they have a lot of qualities, which would make them a good friend if only you gave them the courtesy of a chance.

The Minnesota oration ended with thunderous applause and a standing ovation. Afterward, a mother contacted me to say, "This was the first time my son came home and voluntarily told me about what happened during his day. I am wondering if you would let us fly you back to Minnesota next year to talk at my synagogue, Temple Israel. We are the largest synagogue in Minnesota, with about two thousand families. We also have a high percentage of autistic children in the congregation."

Even with the lingering euphoria of a successful performance, the hotel rooms are always lonely. I've also learned to avoid CNN because nothing is more of a happiness bandit than government bailouts, global warming, species annihilation, natural disasters, infanticide, the Octomom, exorbitant debt, hate crimes, and our former president George W. Bush receiving more than $100,000 to lecture on his eight years of caustic ineptitude. Sometimes I think of Uncle Justin in those sterile hotel rooms . . . wishing he were still around to appreciate my adult accomplishments. Furthermore, his arsenal of nostalgic tapes and games would surely calm my nerves.

As adults, Uncle Justin and I tote bouncy balls in our pockets and order bizarre crap through the mail. (With the help of Amazon.com, I have procured chocolate-covered mealworms, gel ant farms, a butterfly habitat, and a children's ATM bank.) If Uncle Justin and I do share an Asperger's diagnosis, his case was mercifully benign. At the very least, he was spared much of the social

misery that has always haunted me, and he was always surrounded by close friends or beautiful girlfriends. He began losing
his academic motivation, however, around the same age as those
middle school students I recently inspired. My grandmother once
felt her teenage son needed a therapist, but my grandfather immediately rejected the suggestion. Grandpa Bob belonged to a
generation where mild disabilities and learning differences were
not yet recognized by our educational system as genuine impair-
ments. Well, maybe they were recognized, but with more infor-
mal labels: "stupid," "lazy," "unmotivated," etc. During my
uncle's childhood, society was barely on the threshold of understanding that conditions like dyslexia and ADHD were not a fair
representation of a person's intelligence or potential. The most
profound example will always be Albert Einstein—a name synonymous with infinite genius. But Einstein was such a mediocre
student that his teachers suggested he milk cows for a living.

In his early thirties, Uncle Justin experienced an overall lethargic degeneration. One day, he quit working at a popular Las
Vegas hotel and never searched for another job. We have absolutely no idea how he survived or milked out the thousands of
dollars saved from tips. While his Taoist-like lifestyle disturbed
my grandparents, I still considered him to be the coolest adult on
the planet. A few years after my family visited him in Las Vegas,
we received an email asking us never to contact him again. I may
build up much larger audiences in the future, but I will always
scan in vain for Uncle Justin's face. We know he is still alive, but
have absolutely no idea what he is doing or how he manages to
pay his rent.

Regardless of whether my audience is composed of Asperger's
students or neurotypicals, I usually don a candy cane–colored
court jester hat with jingle bells affixed to each fabric branch.

And, of course, the ensemble would not be complete without my Homer Simpson slippers. The nonsensical costume is meant to prove a point. Individuals with Asperger's struggle with flexibility and (in my case) feelings of entitlement. If my intentions are good, then I lack empathy for the comfort zones of others and feel entitled to overstep my bounds. Survival among the neurotypicals requires relentless compromise, overanalyzing the situation, and making life just a little more complicated in order to solve the simplest problems.

In my costume, I am pretending to be a gross exaggeration of my inflexible, egocentric self—someone who always flaunted his flamboyant uniqueness and paid a horrific price. My character becomes clinically depressed from watching others enjoy the breaks associated with career advancement and romance. And yet . . . he continues to fail miserably. In his darkest hour of loneliness, the man finally accepts that his social and professional survival must depend on a willingness to conform. He begins acting normal, with one small exception—Halloween. Halloween is his self-proclaimed Asperger's Independence Day, when he is allowed to impose his suppressed weirdness upon humanity. A major dilemma surfaces when he must show up to the job interview of his life . . . on Halloween of all days! I ask the audience, "If I were this guy, would it make any difference that I hiked the Appalachian Trail for pediatric AIDS or that I always do what I say I'm going to do? Or that I have the self-control to only act weird one day out of the year? Or that I disclose about the Asperger's syndrome to my employer? Will any of my life accomplishments matter if I choose to show up wearing a Halloween costume?"

In our credit-card-swiping culture of immediate gratification, we must look beyond the easiest solution. And it is important to bear in mind that Halloween Guy is going to feel fifteen times more entitled to commit professional hara-kiri than a neurotypical individual. Halloween *is* the most sacred day of the year for him, and he has already sacrificed so much to enjoy these twenty-four hours of All Hallow's madness. Laughter sprinkles throughout the audience while I continue to stand in the ridiculous costume and tell the audience how *I* would go about solving the problem. It involves a series of five "easy" steps:

1. Never dismiss a person's problems with the Trio of All-Time Stupid Clichés, such as "Just Let It Go . . . Get Over It . . . Life Is Not Fair." Telling a person to "let go" is essentially disregarding the person's anguish. This well-meaning advice often has the inadvertent effect of encouraging someone to "hold on" even tighter to his or her demons. If "letting go" were that easy, we all would have done it a long time ago. Wouldn't we?

2. Gingerly explain the likely consequences of a person's actions. In the case of Halloween Guy, it would be prudent to let him know that the decision to wear a costume will result in a 98 percent chance of disaster in this already grim job market.

3. Find a way to relate to the person you are trying to help, so as not to give advice from a pedestal. If you have a brief, personal anecdote that relates to the individual's dilemma . . . tell the story.

4. If possible, invest time searching for the elusive compromise and formulate a plan of action. Halloween Guy should make the choice *not* to wear his costume to give himself a fighting

chance. If he wins the position, he will spend six months working on making a good first, second, and fifteenth impression at work. After the six-month anniversary, Halloween Guy must march to his employer's office to deliver a rehearsed speech as well as disclose about his Asperger's syndrome (if he has not already done so). He will explain there is only one day of the year he absolutely cannot work and ask to reserve Halloween six months in advance.

5. If the first four steps do not lead to success, it is prudent to encourage your advisee to "just let it go!" Assume Halloween Guy's employer could renege on his promise to show mercy on Halloween. This boss may be an intolerant jerk, but he sadly has power over Halloween Guy's livelihood. Explain there will be times when it will make no difference when you compromise on the original compromise made six months earlier. There are going to be times when you *have* to let certain things go for the sake of survival.

Constantly feeling as though I had to "let go" and "back off" were not always the right answers for me. In many cases, it planted the seeds for future bitterness, especially when desperately trying to placate other people. In actuality, I would end up pleasing absolutely nobody (or at least no one who mattered). I would "back off" until I had practically backed myself off the face of the earth. Worst of all, I would start to "let go" of the energy that makes me incredible with the potential to alter my unfair realities.

A BRUSH WITH HOLLYWOOD

There is something magical about movie stars. I experienced this firsthand during a brief, but titillating, encounter in Grand Central Terminal on my way home from co-teaching a class of college-aged Asperger's students (further validating the expression "Those who cannot do . . . teach") in December of 2008. I was trying to take my mind off the realization that I had accidentally left a bottle of my caffeine pills in a classroom and would be fired in one week.

Grand Central's black coffee and Christmas laser show had the psychotropic effect of making me forget about my stupidity, as I began scanning the crowd for high school acquaintances. Ever since I was a young child, one of my talents has been a striking memory for people's faces. (At a doctor's office I once recognized a former teacher at my old elementary school whom

I had only spoken to twice in my entire life and not seen for seventeen years. And inside a local pizzeria, I was the only one in my family who noticed Mary Tyler Moore was sitting at the adjacent table with her much-younger husband whose name I had also memorized.) On this particular day, one face stood out more prominently than the other New Yorkers rushing around Grand Central Terminal. It had an aura of energy that could not be ignored.

"Excuse me?" I stammered. "Are you an actor?"

The man told me he was.

"Yes! I knew it was you! You were that guy in the Harrison Ford movie. You know . . . *Regarding Henry*! You played the lawyer who was friends with Harrison Ford's character."

I introduced myself and shook hands with one of the most popular supporting actors in Hollywood: Bruce Altman.

His hair was grayer, but his trademark voice was just what I remembered from many movies over the years. He has built up a successful career portraying characters who are likeable assholes—gregarious charmers who sleep with their friends' wives (*Regarding Henry*), deliberately undermedicate their psychiatric patients (*Matchstick Men*), and exploit a girlfriend's son (*Rookie of the Year*).

Unlike the characters he often portrays, Mr. Altman seemed to be a genuinely nice person who was interested in getting to know me. He asked what brought me to New York City.

"I'm teaching a Bronx class for high school students about to enter college," I replied with an exaggerated air of importance. "I am also writing a memoir titled *Atypical*."

His follow-up question about what made me atypical was obviously loaded, so I filtered any rogue honesty threatening to escape my lips while mentally ticking off my flaws. *I amuse my-self by loudly farting in voting booths . . . My persistence is so overbearing that girls misconstrue it as stalking . . . I have an Oedipal tendency to embark on sexual relationships with women old enough to be my mother . . . I chronically force my unwanted friendship on others . . .* Instead I gave him the most neutral an-swer I could think of: "I have Asperger's syndrome and hope to use my book to educate people."

Mr. Altman had heard of Asperger's and said he couldn't tell I had it.

"Exactly!" I replied. "There are a lot of people like me, but nobody ever hears about us or our positive qualities."

When Mr. Altman had to step aside to make a phone call, I stood nearby, struggling to maintain equilibrium while my legs turned into rubbery stilts. The epileptic seizure–inducing Yuletide rhapsody had returned and Santa Claus was now gyrating on the ceiling. But I took very little notice. When meeting someone fa-mous, it's easy to forget they are just as human and flawed as the rest of us. We also nurse the fantasy that these chance encounters will blossom into full-blown friendship. I opened my mouth to ask Mr. Altman for his cell phone number and whether I could buy him lunch at T.G.I. Friday's the following week. But luckily my anemic common sense kicked in at the last possible second to remind me that asking a celebrity for such personal informa-tion might not be appropriate. So I asked for his email address instead.

He spelled out his email, which I recorded into my cell phone with jittery fingers. Then, I stared at his email address for five minutes, as though a benevolent sprite from some Roald Dahl fantasy had handed me a magic orb. In a future email, perhaps he would listen to at least some of the questions on my mind that day. I wanted him to tell me why movies about autistic characters peaked in the 1980s, but are now virtually obsolete.

Bruce Altman hopefully understands how important he and his Hollywood brethren are to the survival of my species. After all, a movie would be the most effective medium to shower Asperger's on the world and make an enormous dent in the negative stereotype. Raise the decibel level to something louder than a whisper. Do for Asperger's what *Philadelphia* did for HIV/AIDS. Bruce Altman replied to my one email, and we unfortunately lost contact, as was expected.

I was only seven years old at the conclusion of the 1980s and was too young to appreciate its beauty. The decade was pure magic—the first personal computers, the Disney Channel (before it turned to tween, bubblegum excrement), Indiana Jones, family-friendly sitcoms, John Hughes coming-of-age sentimentality, the birth of MTV, Voodoo Reaganomics, and even the fleeting romanticization of autism. Toward the end of the 1980s, the American moviegoing public experienced a brief, intense fascination with the autistic savant.

> *We're all special. We're all a little like Eric. Maybe*
> *we can't soar off into the clouds. But somewhere . . .*
> *deep inside . . . we can all fly.*
>
> —THE BOY WHO COULD FLY (1986)

The Boy Who Could Fly is a fantasy film about a teenager named Millie who takes an interest in the strange boy next door,

Eric. Eric mostly sits on his windowsill flapping his arms like a wounded bird. He lives with his alcoholic, neglectful uncle as the threat of institutionalization haunts the household. It is safe to assume the pair connected over tragedy, because Eric has lost both his parents in a plane crash and Millie's father recently committed suicide. Telepathy is not classified as an autism symptom, but the movie indicates that Eric began flapping his arms the exact second when his parents died.

Despite living in his own world, Eric bonds with Millie and mimics her facial expressions. For the first time in his life, he experiences the emotions associated with romance and friendship. In Eric, she finds a friend who will never judge her or offer unfair criticism (constructive or malicious). This is perhaps the only movie in which a romantic connection blossoms between a significantly autistic character and a neurotypical protagonist. (A passionate kiss is exchanged on a cloud after Eric flies to Millie's windowsill.)

According to the DSM-IV, psychologically induced aviation is also *not*, in fact, a common symptom of autism. The movie is typical 1980s fantastical fluff with quasi-teen heartthrobs and primitive special effects—a forgettable composite of *Peter Pan* and *E.T.* Even 1988's *Rain Man* is not invulnerable to criticism, because it too was painted with Hollywood varnish as well as Oscar-ized. Furthermore, the movie has evolved into a cultural term like "catch-22" and "The Frankenstein Monster." "Rain Man" is a generic, somewhat offensive, term used by the neurotypical public when describing an autistic individual who has some basic communication skills.

Rain Man was, however, the first mainstream movie to introduce the enigma of autism to a neurotypical public. It is a touching story about the love and admiration that gradually develops between two severely dissimilar brothers, Charlie and Raymond—one of whom is an autistic savant. Charlie quickly realizes that his attempts to manipulate his brother are useless when pitted against Raymond's cemented rituals. Coercion is as effective as gnats trying to smash through Plexiglas. Poor Raymond is the perfect tool because he lacks the mental cognizance to fight back or even realize he's been victimized. As he comes out of his shell—gambling and gaining admirers, kissing and dancing with a woman—we are given a glimpse into the complexities of autism. While many individuals on the spectrum live in their own universe, they also maintain some desire to be included in the neurotypical world.

An estimated 10 percent of the population can be identified as savants. The screenwriter for *Rain Man* modeled Raymond after a real autistic savant named Kim Peek. As for Dustin Hoffman, he received coaching from the autistic cattle-chute designer Temple Grandin (who is currently a tenured professor at Colorado State University). She taught him how to play the part with as much realism and dignity as possible.

Cinematic autism grew progressively mediocre after the blockbuster success of *Rain Man*. The movies were more stereotypical, less poignant, and forgettable, as the autistic individual was portrayed as an impenetrable physiological computer. Even the action movie genre made a half-assed attempt to experiment with autism, in the 1998 commercial failure *Mercury Rising*. But it is not entirely fair to make a knee-jerk judgment by *skriticizing* (I mean, criticizing) these films as having done more harm than good.

Maybe we need to step back in order to analyze these movies from a broader perspective and be diplomatic enough to give their creators some credit. Because a common thread is woven throughout all these movie plots. All the autistic characters tremendously benefit from the love and/or support of at least one neurotypical individual. Autistic individuals may live in their own world, but it is not always the disability holding them back. They need a neurotypical audience to embrace them and take the "radical step" of giving them a chance. And finally, these movies planted ungerminated seeds, which would be revived from dormancy as we learned more . . . While these movies were noticeably flawed and did more justice to Hollywood than to the autistic community, they were one hell of a good start!

Americans have traditionally flocked to movies featuring Rambo/ James Bond–type action heroes. We enjoy movies where the protagonists are a little more physically attractive, heroic, brawnier, and cooler than the rest of us. They barely cheat death and dodge bullets like genetically engineered mosquitoes. We are delusional to think we could ever adhere to these standards, however. Even the actors themselves are probably nothing like their alter egos. It is merely an illusion perpetuated with the aid of stunt doubles and invisible safety harnesses.

People need movies about "losers" as fervently as they want a superhero with a ninja-like wit and reflexes. The term "loser" in this case is a nonoffensive term used to describe someone magnetic toward failure (usually through no fault of their own). Nature does not bestow many breaks on these people with regards to physical appearance and intrinsic talent. Therefore, they have been transformed into walking petri dishes that cultivate ineptitude. And trying to surmount their obstacles is like pouring gratuitous volumes of gasoline on a raging tire fire, accelerating the frequency of failure. This is why we loyally watch the bumbling antics of Steve Carell and Will Ferrell—their personas make us feel better about our own shortcomings. (I did realize *my* life could be much worse after viewing *The 40-Year-Old Virgin*.)

I want more screenwriters and directors to have the progressive wisdom to tap deeper into the autism vein. After all, an Asperger's protagonist would make an incredible, albeit unorthodox, hero. Unlike the large handful of movies featuring characters with profound cases of autism, a cinemaphile must squint in vain when searching for a lone Asperger's protagonist. The first movie that comes to mind is the obscure 2005 film *Mozart and the Whale*, which is a romance between an ornithologically obsessed mathematical genius and a flighty, mentally unstable young woman who both have Asperger's syndrome. Despite casting popular actors and hiring a *Rain Man* screenwriter, the film failed to procure a mainstream audience. The second movie, *Adam*, is a fictional account of an Asperger's protagonist who must fend for himself after his father/caregiver passes away. He develops a romantic relationship with his attractive, upstairs neighbor, who cautiously reciprocates his amorous intentions. While this critically acclaimed movie had a limited theatrical release, it is a harbinger for something more profound than societal tolerance. Acceptance. Acceptance of AS individuals as potential friends, coworkers, employees, and, of course, romantic partners.

In reality, we have already seen Asperger's in the cinema on countless occasions. We just have to go back and take another look . . .

One of my cherished, childhood staples is the 1985 cult film

Pee-wee's Big Adventure. People always refer to it as a cult movie, which just means it is too incredible to be appreciated by everyone. Its protagonist is a flamboyantly eccentric, effeminate, childlike man who exhibits several Asperger's symptoms—most prominently his "restricted, stereotyped patterns of behavior." Pee-wee is obsessed with his vintage bicycle, which is stolen by a spoiled neighborhood bully. Most "adults" would have chalked it up to a painful loss and quickly moved on with their lives. Pee-wee refuses to take this step, however. Losing a bicycle *is* the end of the world, so he embarks on a blindly obsessive cross-country pursuit to retrieve the contraption. His determination and child-like naiveté are irrational (even for someone with AS). God! The man makes a pilgrimage to Texas when a seedy soothsayer says, "Your bicycle is in the Alamo. In the basement!" Pee-wee's emotional problems are then exacerbated after he travels thousands of miles only to learn that the Alamo was built without a basement!

And then there is *The Waterboy*. In this film, the main character, Bobby, is a socially inept "water distribution engineer" who is a tragic stereotype of an AS adult. He is thirty-one years old, but still lives with his overbearing mother, who prefers he not make the effort to surmount his shortcomings. A lifetime of social failures has filled a well of suppressed anger to the brink of explosion.

> *You see, Bobby. You do not have what they call,*
> *eh . . . the social skills. That's why you have never*
> *had any friends. Except for your mama!*
>
> —BOBBY'S MOTHER

Like Pee-wee, Bobby has an intense fixation on one thing (H_2O). He has also endured relentless humiliation over two decades, but continues to tolerate the abuse. This is not the result of innate cowardice, and unlike in real life, we are offered flashbacks into Bobby's childhood psyche before we pass judgment. When Bobby did try fighting back as a child, he was harshly reprimanded. Because AS individuals are challenged by "generalization," Bobby believes the opinions of one ignorant moron are applicable to every single confrontation for the remainder of his life. When Bobby is encouraged to fight back, his circumstances finally change. He is lauded as a hero, which is the ultimate fantasy for many people with Asperger's syndrome.

And finally, let's not forget fifteen-year-old Max from the quirky 1998 comedy *Rushmore*. Our first impression of Max is that he is a selfish jerk with self-inflicted miseries. His grades are extremely poor because studying purloins attention away from his plays, clubs, and miscellaneous projects. While most adolescents are pining after the homecoming queen, Max has an inclination toward women in their thirties to early forties. (Does any of this sound familiar yet?!) On a related note, he displays a prominent Asperger's symptom of developing peer-inappropriate relationships because the younger kids look up to him while adults admire his brilliance and gravitas. All of Max's endeavors (with the exception of academics) must entail over-the-top stunts, and he never knows when to stop. All things unnecessary . . . are always necessary. I cringed throughout most of *Rushmore* because Max is the cinematic manifestation of my own dark side. I could identify with his profound feelings of entitlement, arrogance, obsessive romantic conquests, and general lack of respect for boundaries. The traits have always served to justify the public's contempt for Asperger's syndrome as a character flaw—a defect deserving to be countered with rejection and/or brutal criticism.

We can scrounge up countless adjectives to describe these fictional movie personalities: obsessive-compulsive, overly aggressive, overly passive, passive-aggressive, vindictive, quirky, brilliant, determined, neurotic, angry, frustrated, idiot savants, or lost souls. These fictional entities, however, are given more of a chance than a typical AS individual in the real world. And moviegoers devote at least ninety minutes of their time trying to unravel their enigmatic psyches. By the end of these films, the neurotypical audience admires the character's courage and may even identify with some of his struggles. Pee-wee Herman, Max Fischer, and Bobby Boucher are all extremely dissimilar characters who share a handful of universal truths. They are too high functioning to be considered disabled, while too odd to be judged as normal.

They all nurse the same desperation to connect with their neurotypical peers and escape from a chronic social isolation. They are prepared to chase these goals through sheer determination, manipulation, overcompensation, and even allowing themselves to be exploited. Upon the culmination of these movies, they cease to be "losers" and find redemption as heroes. Furthermore, their success could never have come to fruition without a handful of neurotypical supporters who give them a chance.

Our knee-jerk reaction is to dismiss these characters as fictional entities and assume they just manifested themselves out of thin air. But these characters are man-made and someone had to breathe life into them. Therefore, maybe it is prudent to reexamine the real-life geniuses crouching behind the scenes . . . bringing sentience to their imaginary characters like muppeteers from the Jim Henson Creature Shop.

*   *   *

My second brush with fame was with a Hollywood star who is actively involved in the autism community—legendary actress Sigourney Weaver—at a GRASP (Global and Regional Asperger Syndrome Parnership) luncheon in May 2008. She was casually dressed and had just entered a realm far away from the cattiness of Joan Rivers/Hollywood Gossip/Fashion Trendiness. Sigourney was hanging out with us to accept her Neurotypical of the Year Award, and I experienced the same giddy sensation as I had with Bruce Altman. We idolize celebrities not just because of their talent, but because they have lived out most of our fantasies. The stardust always rubs off with a simple handshake, just a little bit.

In her 2004 movie *Snow Cake*, Sigourney Weaver portrays a woman who has a profound case of high-functioning autism. Ms. Weaver extensively researched the role by actually living in an autistic community, being coached by a woman with autism, and attending GRASP support group meetings. (Nobody at the meetings cared that she was a movie star until they learned she had played Lieutenant Ripley in the *Alien* franchise.) Many actors, after they have wrapped up a project, cease to remain involved in a cause. They move on to new commitments that take center stage in their personal and professional lives. Sigourney Weaver, however, decided to "perseverate" a little bit longer. As I watched her deliver the acceptance speech, I felt like bursting into tears of relief upon realizing this is no publicity stunt. Sigourney Weaver is the rare celebrity who understands that the most profound disablers are the lack of understanding and chances allotted by the neurotypical public. She knows this from her thespian pursuits as well as personal experience. More important, in her acceptance speech Sigourney Weaver confirmed something I had suspected for years:

"Have you ever sat in on a Hollywood board meeting? With all the nail-biting, ticks, stimming, and hand-flapping that goes on at the table . . . I am almost positive half of Hollywood must have Asperger's disorder!"

A GRAVE SITUATION

Don't let the bastards wear you down.

—DR. ROBERT ERNEST COLBY

My mother and father have allowed me to remain in their home even though I am nearly thirty years old. In exchange for rent and food, I perform chores like grocery shopping and household maintenance. But my post-college adulthood coincided with the end of financial support for nonessentials like beer, weekend excursions, and an expensive Beetlejuice costume for Halloween. Therefore, when my parents did lend me money, it was always in the form of an interest-free, verbal credit card repaid in weekly installments once I found employment. Even during spurts of infantilism, I was usually good about turning off the syndicated episodes of *Full House* and searching for a job. They never let me use my disability as an excuse for unemployment, even though my options were never ideal. Almost all of my short-lived careers were either an insult to my education or aggravated my Asperger's neuroses. In so many words, they let me know I'd have to earn my own money even if this entailed joining the circus to shovel elephant shit into a durable plastic bag. But some of the most menial jobs were fortified with fewer social minefields because the risk for failure was not as ominous.

My salvation came in the most unlikely of places when I was intrigued by a CNN broadcast about "recession-proof jobs" that have no chance of being shipped overseas. We needed people in these jobs because they satisfied a societal need that could not and would never . . . die.

The report said that more young people were pursuing jobs in hairdressing and mortuary science. Hairdressing seemed about as realistic as shaving my bikini zone and joining the lineup of the Rockettes. Plus, I was still chipping away at an old $1,500 loan from my parents, and my substitute teaching assignments would be ending in nine days. Taking the entire summer off would have been fiscal suicide. So I grabbed the Yellow Pages and started circling phone numbers for all the local funeral homes.

I felt a surge of euphoria as I set up the interviews, because deep down I knew this was the answer to my prayers. At long last, I had found the fabled golden goose . . . a treasure illuminated by the neon terminus of some rainbow. This would be a more stable environment, with some job security—unlike my substitute teaching assignments, where it was common to be terminated at the drop of a hat. Firing me would force them to scour the community for another employee willing to handle decomposing human remains or cadavers with their entrails spilling out. Individuals with such a morbid constitution do not grow on trees, even during a global recession. If I did get fired from this new job, it would have to be from gross incompetence or maybe embezzlement. Five minutes into my first interview I was told, "Thanks! You're hired and start tomorrow." Just as I had hoped, they were in serious need of help, even if the help happened to be from *me*.

The most challenging aspect about working in a funeral home, for me, is keeping tight control over what I say. On my first day, I asked my supervisor, "Is there anything I *should not* do or say while I'm working in this environment?" Her response amounted to "If you have to ask, then this is probably not the right place for you." I promptly explained about my "situation" as well as how difficult it is for me to automatically shift gears in new environments. She thanked me for being honest, and things have gone pretty smoothly ever since.

It took only two weeks for my flamboyant dialogue to shrivel into four bland phrases:

Welcome . . .

Good-bye . . .

The nearest bathroom is the first door around the corner . . .

I'm sorry for your loss.

Everything else threatened to explode from my lips like Verbal Courier Pigeons from Hell. I learned not to elaborate on what goes on in the embalming room, even when visitors were curious about what my job was like. For example, I could have told them that the movie *Weekend at Bernie's* is completely unrealistic. In real life, the rate of decomposition for an unembalmed body is so relentless that such a farce would be impossible. The stench would be unbearable, and even the most self-absorbed, partying moron would come to the conclusion that Bernie had expired. The smell of death is unique and overpowering.

At first glance, the embalming room resembles a hospital room, except more sterile and depressing. The neck is propped up with half-moon stands at such a distorted angle that you reflexively want to adjust it out of concern for the new "client." It eventually would sink in that the person in front of me did not mind that his neck was craned into a position that would be severely uncomfortable for the rest of us who maintain a pulse. Or that the table was ice cold.

I tried convincing my supervisors to promote social responsibility by opening their doors to high-risk teenagers. Most youths maintain a delusional belief that they are invincible, but my guests would be the absolute extreme—the ones who play Russian roulette with their lives every Friday night by driving with a 1.6 blood alcohol level and ingesting capsules of Ecstasy like damn Tic-Tacs. Some of them are suicidal because they have yet to understand that there is more to life than high school. My funeral home tour would scare them straight.

The tour would conclude in the embalming room:

"This is where you end up after you die. It's not pretty, and one of two things will happen to you. You will either be burned to ashes or make one final appearance before decomposing in the ground forever. The girl you see before you is only seventeen years old. Just four days ago she was laughing with you at the mall. Out of respect, we are keeping her covered while you guys are here. But when we work on the bodies they are usually stark naked. Now . . . would you really feel comfortable having somebody *like me* staring at you as you lie naked on this table?"

I would emphasize *like me* with dramatic, screeching overtones like Joan Crawford in *Mommie Dearest*. Then I would bulge out my eyes as though attempting a grotesque impression of Rodney Dangerfield while flapping my hands like a distressed parakeet. My audience would look away in disgust and answer the question by shaking their heads in unison. Furthermore, my hideous facial expression and the words *like me* would haunt the teenagers whenever their speedometer needle crept toward 80 miles per hour. Or the next time someone was tempted to inject a potent substance into their veins. For once, my creepiness and inappropriate behavior would be harnessed for the benefit of humanity!

As part of my crash course in what not to say, I quickly realized that not every bald white man would find it complimentary to hear that he bore a striking resemblance to James Carville. On a similar note, not every family would laugh as I spun a black golf umbrella at the graveyard while crying out, "Hey! Look at me, everybody! I'm the Penguin from *Batman*!"

There would be a chance some families would appreciate my humor. But not a good chance.

While the funeral home would never turn away a family due to their religious beliefs, they specialized in Roman Catholic funerals. My job required me to attend church services where I routinely made a fool of myself. For some godforsaken reason, Jews show their reverence toward the Lord by standing at least ten times throughout a standard synagogue service. Therefore, I became elated upon noticing a padded, retractable bar by my feet and wondered why this device did not exist in Jewish houses of worship. But even I could have figured things out by taking notice of half the congregation . . . kneeling! The embroidered bar absorbed the mud from my dress shoes as I all but cried out, *"Oh, sweet! A footrest!"*

When it comes to unfamiliar social situations, my family and sympathetic peers have always instructed me to pay attention to what everybody else is doing in order to figure out what's appropriate. So I marched up to the pulpit to graciously accept that tasteless wafer without understanding that Communion is a privilege reserved for practicing Catholics. The priest's upper lip curled as he said, "This is the body of Christ."

"Okay. Thanks!"

Only once did I preside over the funeral of someone younger than forty, who had died very unexpectedly of a heart attack. I knew better than to ask the family too many questions, but I still wanted to know how such a vibrant, healthy man could die so suddenly.

I hope to eventually die from the most unnatural causes at a very old age. My spectacularly bizarre death would ideally take place before the appearance of some terminal illness lurking around the corner, but after my quality of life has already diminished. I want to be the ninety-year-old man who bends down to stroke his sleeping calico cat and has his neck swiped by the startled beast's untrimmed claws. The momentum would be swift enough to sever my jugular vein and cause me to bleed to death in ten minutes like a gushing cistern. The authorities would find a slightly dehydrated cat and a circular pattern of paw prints stained in blood. The detectives would take my cat away to be adopted as their precinct mascot, as they continued investigating my death as a possible homicide. Mainly out of disbelief that such a sweet animal could be responsible for such a grisly death.

Another option would have to be Disney World, which would hopefully give me the courtesy of an equally freakish death. I will make one final pilgrimage to the Magic Kingdom when I'm a decrepit octogenarian. The chances of getting killed at a Disney theme park are so minute that a sensible person does not waste energy thinking about it. But even a 1 out of 150 million chance is still an accident waiting to happen, and I'd like to be around for it. Specifically, I will board the Dumbo ride on the day when the accelerator gears finally jam, causing the pistons to fire in hyperdrive. The ride will spin fifty times its normal speed, my harness mechanism will fail, and I'll be ejected into the sky. But I would hope to be dead before making a trajectory into the adjacent It's a Small World and drowning in its man-made river.

After a lifetime of guzzling nostalgic Disney movies as if to quench some untreatable chronic thirst, to die under those circumstances would be the ultimate irony, like Dan Aykroyd's Stay Puft Marshmallow Man destructor in the first *Ghostbusters* movie, or like the patriarchal mobster played by the late Paul Newman in *Road to Perdition*. I want the chance to look into the eyes of my assassin and whisper, "I'm glad it's you . . ."

Everybody is eventually murdered by time, although it would be incredible to die on my own terms.

I took a monthlong leave of absence from the funeral home when it began draining me of the vitality needed for other endeavors. The inner vigilance required to control my mouth was a succubus of energy at a time when my public speaking career also demanded attention. I often needed a beer at the end of the night, which dulled my frazzled nerves and exacerbated lethargy. Taking some time off turned out to be a wise decision, because my maternal grandfather succumbed to the late stages of Alzheimer's disease just a few weeks later. By then I had regained the energy to prepare for yet another funeral—this time as a grieving family member. My grandmother even asked me to write the eulogy.

Those of you who have had the honor of knowing my grandfather, Dr. Robert Ernest Colby, have witnessed the impact of his illness over the past few years. Alzheimer's is slow, but relentless. His decline happened so gradually that I cannot even recall when he began to say my name with a hint of surprise in his voice—as though he was seeing me for the first time all week or briefly emerging from a murky fog. Yet those of you who have known him for a long time understand that he was still your friend, brother, father-in-law, father, and husband. And, of course . . . he was still my grandfather. Alzheimer's did not delegate much mercy, but the one thing it left alone was his incredible personality and spurts of outrageous humor.

All of you have your own memories of Robert Colby, but I'd like to share a few of my own. I recall my family's incredible visits to my mother's childhood home in New City, New York. As we pulled out of their driveway at the end of each visit, my grandfather and grandmother would run alongside our car as they waved good-bye to us. Once in a while, they would even chase us down the street as they continued waving! I think this is how my entire family felt. We wanted to chase after the magic even if it only bought us a few more minutes.

When I was much younger, my grandfather was the one who took my sister, Dena, and me to extravagant video arcades and the beach during our visits to Florida. As an adult, I learned these environments were absolute torture for him and my grandmother. But he knew these places made us happy, and that was all that mattered to him. I also remember one sunny Florida afternoon when he and I challenged two other boys to a basketball game using the new ball he bought me.

Eventually, Alzheimer's took away his youth and athletic prowess, which lingered well into his seventies. My father once said to me, "There was always one person I could never beat in a tennis match, no matter how hard I tried. It was your Grandpa Bob!" During my childhood visits to Florida, my grandfather introduced me to the game of tennis. He spent a fortune on my lessons and taught me what it feels like to be victorious once in a while. He liked making people happy, but learned a long time ago that trying to please the entire world is about as effective as using a wineglass to bail out the *Titanic*. He would share his own philosophy with my sister, Dena, and me. "I would like . . . I would not like." Most important, my grandfather found joy in our accomplishments.

We knew for a while that this day was inevitable, although our sadness would have been much more profound if not for the love and devotion of my grandmother. She worked tirelessly to make it possible for him to remain in the comfort of his beautiful Delray Beach home long after many spouses would have given up and surrendered to a nursing home. His wonderful aide, Maguy, became part of our family while assisting in his daily care for the last two years. Going above and beyond the call of duty, she has been a tremendous source of comfort and support for my grandmother.

This is my first visit to Florida in almost thirty years that has not been synonymous with profound joy . . . even during the very late stage of his condition. I would like to thank everybody here today for taking the time to pay their final respects to my grandfather. Hopefully some of your memories are just as incredible as mine, and you will hold some of them in your souls forever.

Alzheimer's disease invaded his mind like some ocean commanded by a vengeful Poseidon. Its tsunami-like waves grinded against all brain matter until he had nothing left except amiable dialogue with the "strange faces" that were his family. A stroke took away the rest of his limited mobility, and like a malevolent shape-shifter . . . his dementia finally morphed into a machete that amputated everything else. When my grandmother made the decision to remove the feeding tube . . . there was nothing left to take except an empty shell artificially clinging to mortality.

My grandfather's interment inside a Delray Beach mausoleum was fascinating and unlike any burial ritual I had ever experienced at my funeral home. His body was hoisted toward the ceiling with machinery that was a cross between a church truck and cherry picker. Funeral workers pushed his casketed body into a quadrilateral chamber before an engraved, marble square was cemented over the horizontal opening. I turned to someone behind me and abandoned the robin-thin eggshells of decorum.

"Oh, God," I whispered. "This is, like, one of the coolest things I've ever seen in my life! I've always wondered how they lift the dead people so high in a mausoleum." She chuckled (I think).

Back at my grandmother's house there was catering and anecdotes about Grandpa Bob's antics. I probably could have lived without hearing about the times he exercised stark naked at a men's health club while reading the *Wall Street Journal,* but I laughed once the shudders dissipated. The story also stirred a long-repressed memory of the time when he took me to a health spa at his former country club. All the elderly gentlemen walked around without a hint of shame as I felt trapped in some homoerotic Garden of Eden for the Damned. And the sight of shriveled testicles exposed like deflated balloons was so perturbing that I ended up wading into the hot tub still wearing my bathrobe.

The deaths of loved ones are solemn occasions not typically

synonymous with pleasurable activities. It is also customary to remain in the house for at least one day to honor a loved one's memory in accordance with Talmudic law and just plain common sense. Many Jews perform a weeklong ritual of mourning called sitting shiva, in which they avoid hedonistic activities, light candles, and cover up all the mirrors. But my grandfather's funeral took place in late September, when Florida still boasted ninety-five-degree afternoons, after a rainy, unseasonably cold mess of a summer back north. Just three minutes down the road, a lukewarm pool was emitting Harpy-like pheromones as though taunting me for squandering a beautiful day. My poor grandfather had been shoved into his alabaster tomb no more than three hours earlier, but I was about to regress two decades and cave into my base, childish impulses.

I announced to my mother, "I'm going to get changed and go swimming at the club!"

My mother sighed, "Jesse, this is not a vacation! I do not think it is appropriate to do something like that today. You can go swimming in the morning."

I performed a quick scan of the house. My father was playing Texas Hold-'em on the Internet and I could hear the chimes of text messaging from my sister Dena's cell phone. My eighty-one-year-old grandmother was handling her new widowhood with unexpected resiliency and maybe a touch of relief. As she kept herself busy in the kitchen, I did not get the impression she needed or appreciated a houseful of people hovering over her as if she were a porcelain doll.

I shot back, "This is ridiculous! We never go down to Florida. Everyone has left the house, and I'm going swimming."

Dena and my father reluctantly followed my example as we drove to the pool. As it turned out, I had blurted out what everyone else was thinking. It made no sense to squander a beautiful day and deliberately prolong the grief we had already endured as Grandpa Bob disappeared.

The country club was almost completely deserted because many of the winter-bird residents were still in their summer homes. Seventeen years ago, this scene would have been swarming with preteenagers enjoying their family vacations while squabbling over use of the Ping-Pong table. Grandpa Bob would have been in close proximity, with his cognizance restored to its former glory. In those days he occasionally called his grandchildren "Justin and Janis" (the names of his children, my mother and uncle). But we always brushed it off as an absentminded reflex.

Playing Ping-Pong with Dena was like dancing in an empty ballroom without any music on a day we were willing to accept anything at all. Despite not having practiced for at least a year, we were both equally matched, with enough raw talent to keep the ball in play up to three minutes at a time. We actually maintained a conversation in between a sequence of mesmerizing hollow smacks, as I told Dena about a Wii video game in our local Best Buy store.

"You can actually play Ping-Pong as an anime character and manipulate its movements like you're actually holding a paddle!"

My wildest imagination could not have anticipated I'd end up playing Ping-Pong and going swimming subsequent to the funeral of one of my grandparents. But it felt really good! This time I succeeded in ignoring whatever shame did exist because it would only conjure the voices: "Normal people do not do something like this right after their grandfather's funeral. What exactly is wrong with you?! Don't you have any damn respect?" The voices were once profound enough to provoke explosive temper tantrums in the middle of the day when I was left alone in my house. The rage would not subside until after I collapsed on the couch, pounding one fist into the left side of my skull.

I would then embark on yet another dangerous search for approval, only to be bombarded with harsh criticism from the same peers who always condemned my mild autism as a character flaw. But at long last, I no longer gave two shits.

EPILOGUE

After quitting my IBM job, the pain inside me intensified, and the stench around me intensified, too, as I began to shower less frequently. Sometimes I literally wanted to die. True despair comes not only from perpetual failure, but an absence of hope. The accolades from my hike became a waning memory, replaced by fresh bouts of unrelenting failures for at least two years. I anticipated my thirties creeping up like a venomous sloth while I remained faithful to the negative stereotype of an AS adult: chronically unemployed; without a girlfriend or spouse; bitter; lethargic; personal hygiene–challenged; falling asleep at 2 a.m. to Disney movies in my parents' basement; and angry. My perpetual holiday in Loser Land showed me these fears could someday progress into sad realities. I also dreaded the possibility that my goals of marriage and children would never come to fruition.

Eventually, hope would extinguish some of the darkness and linger like the gleaming fireplace embers long after the rest of my family goes to bed. The prospect of writing a book—this book— presented the possibility of a career beyond twelve-hour night shifts at IBM or chronic terminations from substitute teaching positions.

The autism statistics ominously soared after my hike ended; 1 out of 175 children . . . 1 out of 150 children . . . 1 out of 125 children. "More children are diagnosed with autism than AIDS, cancer, and diabetes . . . *combined*." The media consistently used the term "epidemic," as though the diagnosis hovered over mankind like a genetic, post-apocalyptic plague. I, on the other hand, wanted to believe the statistics were inflated by society's recent understanding of autism as a broad spectrum. Before Asperger's syndrome was officially recognized in 1994 in the DSM-IV, many individuals with this condition were promptly dismissed as learning disabled, lazy, weird, socially inept, and stupid. And even though the mercury-based preservative Thimerosol was removed from most vaccinations after 2001, new parents still worry. Now, more than ever, we must embrace stories offering some semblance of hope. It seemed prudent to write a book before our high-speed Internet pop culture moved on to more cosmopolitan topics, or more ambitious writers exhausted the public's attention span.

My literary aspirations were further piqued after my father arranged for me to have lunch with one of his customers who is a legendary sportswriter (who has since passed away). He was a self-made man who lived a life of chances taken and integrity maintained, filled with celebrity encounters (including Babe Ruth, Marlon Brando, and others). While he did not strike me as a lifelong people-pleaser, old age had further grizzled him into speaking his mind without obsessing over taste and decorum. When I shared people's pessimism toward my crackpot endeavors, he gruffly replied, "Fuck 'em!"

My friend told me he liked my newspaper articles and encouraged me to write a book about "everything."

"Write about your accomplishments, your travels, your dreams, your sex life . . ."

In the summer of 2006, I began the frustrating process of sending query letters and self-addressed, stamped envelopes to literary agencies specializing in the nonfiction/memoir genre. After just four days, the first heap of my returned SASEs lurked in the mailbox—affixed with rejection cards and mimeographed form letters. More piles arrived every single day for a solid month. I appreciated how the literary agencies did not use "ignoring" as a form of communication, as so many neurotypicals seem to do. And despite the fusillade of rejections, receiving so much personal mail appealed to my postal inclinations. Finally, seven agencies expressed lukewarm interest and requested the entire book proposal.

Six book proposals made their boomerang journeys in the SASEs I supplied, before I called the final literary agent stringing me along. A woman with a euphonious voice sighed, "Some of it did not work for me."

By this time, I had begun to welcome the rejections as opposed to further torturing myself with false hope. The sweet voice continued, "But other parts were kind of interesting. I wish you wrote more about what it feels like to be *you* instead of just your experience on the Appalachian Trail."

"Look!" I stammered. "Just tell me what you want and give me a chance to write new material. I am someone who *always* does what he says he is going to do!"

"I am well aware of that! If you can show me more of this writing, it is quite possible you will someday have a good book. And I *will* help you."

My book was pieced together in steady increments despite constant writer's block—a real foe for both aspiring and professional writers. An eleven-page chapter would take anywhere from two days to two weeks to compose. Somebody once told me people come up with their best ideas in the bathroom, as I took our nation's BlackBerry-sporting, multitasking Puritan work ethic to an extreme level. Whenever inspiration was stifled, I sat on the toilet to write prose on my PocketMail device so the creative flow would not be interrupted by answering the call of nature. Packages of Play-Doh were purchased from the local pharmacy, which were inhaled like a gorgeous woman's perfume. I also made weekly trips to the Pleasant Valley Library to rent DVDs of *Mary Poppins* and *Chitty Chitty Bang Bang*. The point of this madness was to regress back a few years . . . to a time when reality and fantasy seemed to coexist in homeostatic harmony. I believed retreating to this mental state would stimulate those creative muses. Sometimes these exercises aided with the writing and other times it made no damn difference. My obsession with the postal system also turned into a valuable asset, encouraging me to compose writing every week. A friend from the *Poughkeepsie Journal* became an enthusiastic target as pages of new material were mailed out to him at least three times a week. His three small children compared the experience to the first Harry Potter movie when constant letters from Hogwarts School of Witchcraft and Wizardry terrorized the repulsive Dursley family. For the first time since my hike ended, I felt justified indulging in the same obsessions discouraged by therapists and responsible for alienating people in the past.

Writing a book has turned out to be the hardest endeavor of my life. But eventually, with the guidance of my literary agent, I was able to complete what once seemed an impossible task. With her support, the embers of hope reignited.

My experiences with the mildest form of autism have been anything but mild. And yet I feel blessed that it has been a roller coaster of extreme highs and lows. I've basked in the thrill of being treated like a local celebrity as well as endured the agony of being condemned as a social pariah. While I worry about turning into an inept leader of the Asperger's community who inadvertently directs his flock off a precipice, I won't shirk the opportunity. People just have to be forewarned they are receiving self-help advice from a man who sometimes entertains himself by farting in public and conversing in gibberish to his cats.

My advice for others with AS is optimistic, but realistic. People do judge a book by its cover, and first impressions will be brutal. Well-meaning individuals will provide you with advice and "constructive criticism" that will not always be constructive or fair. (My favorites are "Stop trying so hard" and "Just be yourself.") Therefore, it is often necessary to impose yourself upon the lives of those who come to knee-jerk conclusions about you. Show them who you are and do not be modest about your accomplishments. It would be naive to assume the demons eventually go away, but they may be utilized to one's advantage.

But we also need individuals who are magnanimous enough to give us a chance. Step back and take another look. As society continues to witness the gifts we have to offer, a dramatic expansion of our opportunities and neurotypical allies will follow. Perhaps this is the missing piece of the puzzle we have all been searching for . . .

I began this journey walking over two thousand miles for the

Joey DiPaolo AIDS Foundation. Somewhere along the way, I ended up stepping out for myself and others like me. Perhaps I also succeeded in letting a few things go, especially the part about my Asperger's syndrome being a disability. In actuality, the greatest disabler is being paralyzed by ignorance and intolerance when these realities could be alleviated through making the effort to understand. For the first time in my life, it became possible to look beyond my opaque bitterness and welcome the harbingers of change . . .

ACKNOWLEDGMENTS

It seems unfair to limit my appreciation to only a handful of people when so many own a piece of this book. Regardless of whether you are mentioned, you know who you are.

I owe much of my post-college success to the Joey DiPaolo AIDS Foundation. Joey DiPaolo, you changed the way people judge those with HIV/AIDS and gave me the courage to go public about my struggles with mild autism. Mike Venterola and Carol DiPaolo-Venterola, you gave me the encouragement necessary to walk more than two thousand miles. I'll also never forget the campers and staff of Camp TLC for reminding me that there are some venues where I can be myself.

I owe a huge debt of gratitude to President Mark Gearan and his family for their kindness at such a crucial time. The chances available at Hobart and William Smith Colleges paved the way for a level of success that is atypical for individuals on the autistic spectrum.

There were a number of teachers who encouraged me and treated Asperger's syndrome as anything but a character flaw. They were pioneers when "being really weird" was not considered to be a legitimate disability. A few who come to mind are Joan Storm, Karen Widing, Bruce Bevins, Sharon Wilhelm, Mary Jean Reid, Eric Buergers, Julia Bucklin, Richard Krause, and Sally Wohlbach.

Thank you to Michael John Carley, Sarah Borris, Karl Wittig, and members of the Global and Regional Asperger Syndrome Partnership (GRASP) Inc. You proved something beautiful could still grow from consistent rejections and failures. I hope the impact of *Atypical* will encourage the neurotypical public to take another look at all you have to offer. And a huge thank-you to Sigourney Weaver and Bruce Altman for the personal support they have given me.

A lion's share of appreciation goes out to my agents and friends, Jeff Herman and Deborah Levine Herman. You were the lone light at the end of a tunnel of rejections. Thank you to my outstanding editor, Marian Lizzi, who saw this book's potential and gave me the chance of a lifetime, and to her assistant, Christina Lundy, for tolerating my relentless emails and offering me guidance.

Karl A. Brautigam III, I still don't have a Plan B, but your enduring friendship has sustained me over the years and was critical during my Appalachian Trail hike. Mateo Prendergast, you infused me with a second adolescence after the journey ended. Thanks to all my other hiking partners who remained loyal despite my tenacious eccentricities and bouts of lethargy— Alex Stafford, Jocelyn Scholer, Sandy Price, and Josh England.

And, of course, Dario Malcolm—my longest, most devoted child-hood friend.

There are many unsung heroes who deserve recognition for their contributions. Thank you to Charles Perez, Walter Weigel and Poughkeepsie's Eastern Mountain Sports, Richard Carroll, the Pleasant Valley Copy Shack, my incredible grandmother Brina Colby, Jessy Lazhir and the Daily Planet staff, and Pete Colaizzo.

I'd also like to thank my future, now-imaginary girlfriend who avoided judging me on trivial matters such as wearing socks with sandals or the constant sound of Tic-Tacs jangling in my pockets! So . . . thank you, (insert name here).

And last, but certainly not least, I owe the most appreciation to my parents, Lewis and Janis Saperstein, for their continual, unconditional love and support throughout all my adventures. Thank you for tolerating my decision back in 2004 to put off graduate school, remain in the house, work a twelve-hour night-shift job, and invest my entire bank account into an endeavor with an 80 to 90 percent failure rate. And thank you for tolerat-ing these things all over again in 2006 when I decided to write a book!

ABOUT THE AUTHOR

Photo by Todd Clinton

Photo by Janis Saperstein

Jesse A. Saperstein graduated cum laude from Hobart and William Smith Colleges in Geneva, New York, in 2004 with a Bachelors degree in English and a minor in Peer Education.

Inspired by his work as a residential advisor in an AIDS awareness–themed house, he hiked the entire Appalachian Trail on behalf of the Joey DiPaolo AIDS Foundation. The 2,174-mile endeavor received attention from local and national media, and raised nearly $20,000 for pediatric AIDS and Camp TLC, where Jesse has worked as a volunteer counselor.

Jesse was diagnosed with Asperger's syndrome at age fourteen. He is an advocate and public speaker for autism awareness, and plans to hike the more than 2,600-mile Pacific Crest Trail to benefit autism research. He lives with his family in Pleasant Valley, New York.

Photo by Alex Stafford